Reasons for Duty

by

John H. Gerstner, Ph. D.

Author of
The Rational Biblical Theology of Jonathan Edwards,
Wrongly Dividing the Word of Truth, Jonathan
Edwards: Evangelist, Theology for
Everyman, and *Reasons for Faith*

Soli Deo Gloria Publications
...for instruction in righteousness...

Soli Deo Gloria Publications
P.O. Box 451, Morgan, PA 15064
(412) 221-1901/FAX 221-1902

*

*

ISBN 1-57358-019-8

Dedication

To Bill and Jeanne McKelvey
—two faithful friends in our one faith

Preface

This volume is intended as a companion to *Reasons for Faith* (Harper, 1959, and Soli Deo Gloria, 1995). In some ways it presupposes its predecessor as discussions of ethics usually do presuppose discussions of philosophy and religion. However, we have tried to make the argument for *Reasons for Duty* understandable, if not completely definable, apart from *Reasons for Faith*, just as *Reasons for Faith* is definable, if not completely understandable, apart from *Reasons for Duty*. Each volume intends to be a serious, howbeit non-technical, statement of a case for Christianity.

Contents

Contents

Foreword

"Duty . . . Honor . . . Country"—these were the foci of the memorable speech given by General Douglas MacArthur at West Point decades ago. That speech galvanized a generation of soldiers, provoking in their souls a dedication to duty above life itself.

In the ensuing years something happened to the virtues of duty and honor. Honor has faded into a quaint sentiment that is deemed archaic. Duty has become just another four-letter word, too obscene to be uttered or scribbled as graffiti on the walls of a dying culture.

Ours is an era of unprecedented antinomianism. We are a nation of "scofflaws" where even in the church everyone does what is right in his own eyes. Ethical relativism is like a Siamese twin, joined at the hip with practical atheism. The culture still embraces a theoretical theism but in practice we live as if there were no God. We are fulfilling Dostoevski's axiom: "If there is no God then all things are possible."

John Gerstner knows better. He knows that God is, and that wherever He is there is duty. To have God without duty is impossible. God has the eternal and intrinsic right to impose obligation, to bind the consciences of His creatures. God is no antinomian. He is transcendentally pronomian.

The Gospel frees us from the killing judgment of the Law. It liberates us from the curse of the Law; but it never denigrates the Law of God. The Gospel saves us not *from* duty, but *unto* duty by which the Law of God is established.

This book is both an exercise in ethics and an exercise in apologetics. It is an *apologia* for duty. It answers the question, "Why should I?" with a defense of the answer, "Because God so commands me." It provides a reason for duty. The reason of this work is not a naked form of rationalism, nor a mere exposition of the *lex naturalis*. It is a profound exposition of the Biblical revelation of Law. The Decalogue is explored in the depths of its many facets and nuances. The Law is set before us as a mirror with two sides. One side of the mirror reflects the holiness of God, His own internal righteousness, which is the ground and fountainhead of the good. The other side reflects our unholiness, our sin that drives us to the Gospel wherein we find a righteousness that is not inherently our own, but is an alien righteousness, a righteousness apart from us that is imputed to us and by which we are declared just in the Beloved.

The justified saint is also a being-sanctified saint, a changed person, regenerated and indwelt by the Holy Spirit. The justified person is being molded into conformity to Christ as His craftsmanship. He is being formed into a child of faith who is at the same time a son or daughter of duty, a lover of the Law of God.

This book explains the Law, defends the Law, and shows the sweetness of the Law. It can help us delight in the Law as it was meant to be understood, and to delight in performing our duty to the One whose Law it is.

R.C. Sproul
Orlando
1995

Part 1

Introduction

Chapter 1

The Origin of the Moral Sense

Where do we start? Or when do we start? When do we start to make moral judgments of right and wrong? Surely the baby does not make judgments, moral or otherwise. When does the child begin to make moral judgments? Let us see.

For the first year or so, the parent gives no moral commands to the infant. At least, if the parent does he does not take himself seriously; or, in any case, the child surely does not take him seriously. The child does not know what the parent is talking about, much less whether it is right or wrong, or even what right and wrong can possibly mean. If the child is prone to roll off the bed, the parent does not tell him not to roll off the bed. He simply builds some sort of barricade. And the child does what is right—abstains from rolling off the bed—because there is no possibility of doing otherwise. We presume that he has no feelings of virtue for not rolling off the bed, and no sense of vice if he does escape the barricade. At least, he does not seem to have any, we see no way by which he could have any, and we do not ourselves remember having had any.

Gradually the child grows. Little by little he understands the meaning of words: "bed," "roll," "fall," "don't." He comes to understand that his parents are telling him not to roll off the bed. He even understands some of their reasons. It seems he will hurt himself if he falls off the bed. And that would seem to hurt his parents also, he senses. So he sees some *reasons* for not falling off the bed. Is this tantamount to knowing that he ought not to fall from the bed? that it would be *wrong* to fall from the bed? If so, what is the difference between seeing the hurtfulness of falling from the bed and the wrongfulness of falling from the bed? Let us see if these two notions are not identical.

Suppose the youngster devises a method of falling from the bed without hurting himself—maybe he places a pillow at the point of landing. So now he rolls off the bed at random. While he is playing this little game his parents come in. They are angry. Why? Because he is hurting himself? No, because he is disobeying them. They had not said do not hurt yourself. They had said do not roll off the bed. What angers his parents is not that his action is physically hurtful to him, but that it is an act of disobedience.

Is this then the birth of the moral idea? Is disobedience to parents the definition of the wrong? It may well be in the case of the child. There seems to be no other source of the moral idea. We find no evidence of an innate moral voice which immediately communicates to the child the notion that certain things are right and certain things are wrong, anymore than he has any innate intellectual faculty which defines "right" and "wrong" for him. There is no revelation made to him saying, "Do this" or "Do not do that." There is no discoverable source of moral information except from his adult preceptors, his parents in most cases. If they issue no commands, the child develops no sense of right and wrong. He will presumably learn to avoid certain things because doing them brings pain, or cultivate certain things because doing them brings pleasure. But nothing seems to tell him that the doing of things that bring pleasure is a duty or that the avoiding of things that bring pain is a duty. Nor does he seem to equate the missing out on pleasure or the incurring of pain as morally significant things.

The child, therefore, leads us to the parent. The child himself does not seem to explain the origin of his own sense of morality. Its origin seems directly connected with the teaching of his parents. They tell him that certain things are right and certain things are wrong. He does not know enough to challenge them. He acquiesces in them by default, at least.

Where, then, does the parent receive the knowledge, if such it is, that what it tells the child to do it is a duty to do? Some will answer outright that the Bible, or some Word of God, teaches that children are to honor their father and their mother and, therefore, obedience is a duty.

Can the Bible, or any other religious book, be the source of this sense of morality? Does a knowledge of ought come by divine revelation and only by divine revelation? Apparently not, for several reasons. First, if the Bible, or any special religious literature, is the source of moral consciousness, then the existence of a moral consciousness outside of the Bible or other religious tradition would be left unexplained. Since Christian and/or religious communities have no monopoly on conscience, no literature can be the sole source of this consciousness. Second, the Bible itself teaches that men have a moral consciousness independent of the Bible. Romans 2:14-16, "When the Gentiles, which have not the law, do by nature the things contained in the law, these, not having the law, are a law unto themselves: which shew the work of the law written in their hearts, their conscience also bearing witness, and their thoughts the meanwhile accusing or else excusing one another; In the day when God shall judge the secrets of men by Jesus Christ according to my gospel." So that the Bible points away from itself as the source of conscience. Third, the acceptance of the Bible as the Word of God presupposes a moral conscience. How would we ever come to acknowledge the Bible if we did not possess a conscience in the first place? Someone may say that the evidence for the Bible's inspiration explains its acceptance. We ask: Why should we accept something because it is divinely inspired? It is our sense of ought which constrains us to accept an inspired document, not an inspired document which constrains us to believe in a sense of ought.

We return to our question: Why does the parent suppose that what he commands the child to do the child *should* do? Does the parent have a built-in voice which tells him that he has this authority? We answer in the negative for two reasons. For one thing, parents lay no claim to such a voice. Second, if they did, they would have to explain when it suddenly appeared, for it was not innate as we noticed in our consideration of the child. If we did not bring it with us into the world, and if it is not later given by some external authority, such as the Bible, when did it come and from whence?

We shall have to probe deeper. Let us return to the original situation and go over it again. Perhaps a dialogue will help. The child is now ten, and instead of rolling off the bed he is now prone to fall out of trees. Father has a conversation with him.

FATHER: Son, you must not climb trees.

SON: Why not?

FATHER: Because I say so.

SON: Why should I do what you say?

FATHER: That is an insolent and wicked question.

SON: Why do you call it wicked? It seems like a reasonable question.

FATHER: Because you should respect me as your father; you should obey your father.

SON: Why?

FATHER: *Why?*

SON: Yes, why? Is it because you are a man? an older, stronger man than I am? It cannot be that because you yourself tell me not to do what every man whom I meet tells me to do. Why should I do what you tell me to do?

FATHER: I am not any man, I am your father. That makes a difference.

SON: What is the difference? The fact that you feed and clothe me? If so, should I obey every man who comes along who may offer me food and clothing?

FATHER: No, son, it goes deeper than that. I care for you all the time, and without me you could not live or, at least, not live most advantageously. Nature places human beings in families. That seems to be the way they are intended to live.

SON: Father, what I want to know is why I should obey you, and you tell me that nature seems to indicate obedience on the child's part. How does it indicate it?

Is there some mysterious voice of nature which tells the child: "Obey your parents"? If so, I have never heard it, nor has any other child I know.

FATHER: No, son, there is no such voice as that, nor was that what I meant by saying that nature teaches the obedience of children. But I do admit your point that I was begging the question rather than explaining how nature indicates this obedience.

SON: Well, then, will you explain?

FATHER: Yes, this is what I meant. First, nature obviously intends for men and women to live together and to have children. That is self-evident, as you will someday admit, though I must ask you now to take my word for it. Now nature is very kind in thus ordaining things for such family life, would you not agree?

SON: Yes, I should certainly not want to be without a family.

FATHER: Very well, then, may I ask another question of you?

SON: Surely.

FATHER: If it is good that nature places human beings in families, would you not also suppose that nature means for these families to be harmonious and happy?

SON: Yes, that seems reasonable.

FATHER: Very well, then, does this not require family order? Would the alternative chaos and bedlam not make for disharmony and unhappiness?

SON: Yes, I can see that there must, in the nature of things, be order. But does nature tell us what this order should be?

FATHER: No, not in so many words. But I think that it intimates what this order should be.

SON: How is that?

FATHER: Well, is it not clear that all persons have wishes and wills of their own, and that if these had no control they would necessarily conflict, at least some of the time, if not most of the time.

SON: That seems evident.

FATHER: If there would be conflict, there could not be harmony and happiness which nature, we said, aims at. Could there be?

SON: No, there could not be. I will grant that there must be some order. But how does nature indicate what this order must be?

FATHER: Well, how can we bring harmony into a situation of conflicting wills except by making some will supreme? Can you think of any other way of bringing harmony into conflict?

SON: No, I guess I can't. I know I can't. Very well, granted, then, that there must be authority in the home, how does nature show that it should be your will that should be dominant? Is there some voice which says to you, "Rule your son"? I can hear no voice which says to me, "Obey your parents." How am I to know that this is my duty?

FATHER: Is that really very difficult to discover?

Granted that no voice says, "Obey your parents" any more than any voice says, "Have order in your homes." Still, is there not the same clear intimation in this matter as in the other instance considered? That is, is it not self-evident that one should have authority to rule who is by nature best fitted to rule.

SON: That does seem clear and you need not say more. I admit that you are better fitted to rule than I am; that parents are better fitted to rule than children, at least in most cases. But what about that?

FATHER: What about what?

SON: About the case where the son may know better than his father? You will admit that this is conceivable, will you not? Or at least that it is possible, and even probable, that a child sometimes knows better than his father?

FATHER: Yes, son, I will admit that it is possible and even probable that children sometimes know better than their parents.

SON: Well, then, does not that fact upset your theory?

FATHER: I think not, and for this reason. If the fact that children may sometimes know better than their parents should upset the necessary order of a home, we would revert to that condition of chaos from which order was to deliver us. Every home would be without authority and the inevitable con-flict would ensue. So whatever conclusion we are to draw from the fact that children sometimes know better than their parents, we may not permit this to upset the economy of the home already established. May we?

SON: I can see and grant that, father, but it still seems that some concession should be made to my point.

FATHER: I agree, but the concession must be made within a framework of undisturbed authority. Is that not clear?

SON: But how is that to be done?

FATHER: Parents must be willing to consider the views of their children, especially in areas where the possibility of the children's knowing better than the parents exists. I say "consider," not "yield to." For the parents to yield to their children's opinions would subvert the necessary order of the home. For the parents to consider the views of the children and then make their own decisions on the basis of their own wisdom and authority would do justice to the rights of the child and not jeoparize the authority of the parent.

SON: That seems fair enough.

Does not such a conversation as the above suggest where the ought emerges? Morality is a principle of nature. Conscience is con-scientia: that which goes along with knowledge, the knowledge of things as they are. In the situation discussed, the act of disobedience, conscience does not say in so many words, "Thou shalt not

disobey thy parents." But the human intelligence leads to
that conclusion, and there is something in the constitution of men which confirms it. This something in man
which persuades us that we ought to do what seems wise
to do is something more than that by which we discover
what it is wise to do. To be sure, we cannot know that we
ought to do what it is wise to do unless we first know
what it is wise to do; but the knowing what it is wise to do
is not all there is to knowing that we ought to do what it
is wise to do. Presumably, a person could know what it is
wise to do and not have any feelings about the doing of it.
We know from experience that men do not always do what
seems wise for them to do, but we also know that in that
case they feel that they have done wrong. Compunction
of conscience sets in as a nemesis when the judgment of
intelligence is not obeyed; peace of conscience follows
when the judgment of intelligence is obeyed.

COMPUNCTION -
        THE STINGING OR PRICKING OF THE
CONSCIENCE.

NEMESIS - A GREEK GODDESS PERSONIFYING
    RETRIBUTIVE JUSTICE. ONE WHO TAKES
                        REVENGE

Chapter 2

The Sanctions of Moral Laws

Suppose a college student has no interest in a course or courses. He has no love for study in general and those courses in particular. How do you induce an interest? Well, you do so by getting him to become familiar with the course and discovering that it is really interesting, and that only his indolence, which prevents his greater knowledge, keeps him from realizing it. So let him overcome his disinclination by studying.

But he may reply, "That is the problem. I have no inclination to study, and you tell me to overcome it by studying. You tell me that I will want to know the course if I learn the course, when my very problem is that I don't want to learn the course. To be sure, if I had some knowledge I would probably have the inclination to get more knowledge; but if I do not have the inclination in the first place, how am I going to get the knowledge?"

What do you say to that perfectly logical approach to the problem? The man is right. You cannot beget an inclination by means of knowledge if you need the inclination in the first place in order to get the knowledge. What are you going to do? You must appeal to some other motive. The man is utterly indisposed to getting the knowledge in question. Very well, there is no point in urging him to get what he has no disposition to get. You had better appeal to something for which he does have a disposition. And indeed, schools are constructed to appeal to an ulterior motive. With most people education is always compulsory. Most persons who have come to love learning without being compelled to do so were compelled in the first place.

We all know how this compulsion works. The student must study or else. Sanctions. First, there are spankings, perhaps; later, social stigma and economic loss. The student studies because it is the lesser of the possible evils. As a child he may not like to study, but likes to be spanked even less. As a collegian he may not like to study, but he likes a parental, professorial, or student frown even less, and an inferior job and poorer income least of all. So without any inclination to study, he studies. In some cases this exposure to study "takes." The person learns to love learning for learning's sake. An inclination to study is born. In many other cases, the exposure never takes. Or, if there is any love for study struggling for birth, a love for other things causes an academic abortion.

The religious situation is not greatly different from this pattern. All men—not some men, but all men—are born with an aversion to true religion, to the living God. They are His enemies. They have no relish for Him or His commandments—least of all His commandments. Maybe He would be acceptable if it were not for His commandments. If He did not say "do this" (which we do not want to do) and "don't do that" (which we do want to do), we probably would have no objection to God. If He would only let us do what we want to do and not make us do what we don't want to do, or if He would only leave us alone, He would be an all-right person. But He being as He is and we being as we are, enmity is the inevitable result. Sometimes, I may add as an aside, people demur at this point, saying that they are not at war with God. But when we examine their statement closely we discover that what they mean is this: "We are not at war with the God whom we like to *think* is the true God." That true God turns out to be an idol. When the nature of the true God is pointed out to them, then they say, "Well, if that is what God is like, I have no use for Him at all!"

If men have this disinclination toward God, it will not change the disinclination to tell them that they should not have it. You may send it underground that way. That is, you may make them ashamed to admit that they have it. But you will not remove it that way. If they have it, they have it. They may not continue to admit that they have it, but that does not alter it, of course. Neither will your telling them that it would be better if they felt differently change their feelings. As they feel they feel. If you explain more clearly the nature of the true God on the sentimental theory that they will love God if they know Him better, you will find that they hate Him more—the more that they understand of His true nature.

What do yo do with a person who is more averse to learning about God than most students are to learning about Latin? It appears that you will have to have compulsory religious education also. If men will not learn of God, and learn to love Him willingly, they shall have to do so unwillingly, just as they learn many other things unwillingly without their inclinations being changed.

We know who administers the academic sanctions, but who is able to apply religious sanctions? Persons are not usually spanked for not loving God. They suffer no professorial frown or parental frown or economic frown for not loving Him sincerely for the simple reason that nei-

ther parent, nor professor, nor employer can tell whether
another person truly loves God or not. All they can do is
insist that there must be the outward profession of due
respect for the deity. More than that is hardly in their
power. That much demonstration is easily in the power of
the most confirmed hater of God. As a matter of fact, Psalm
66:3 says that many, because of God's power, "feign
obedience" (margin): "Through the greatness of Thy
power shall Thine enemies submit themselves unto Thee."

What sanctions does the Searcher of hearts impose for
not loving Him with all the heart, soul, mind, and
strength? He afflicts the person with outward adversity.
"The wrath of God is revealed from heaven against all
ungodliness and unrighteousness of men, who hold the
truth of God in righteousness," Romans 1:18. Genesis tells
us that thorns and thistles and the cultivating of the
earth with difficulty was a result of sin and not natural to
the created world. All the calamities, disasters, diseases,
and catastrophes are natural to this world after it had
become a fallen world and not when it was a paradisical
one. Hell is the place where there is nothing but sin and,
therefore, nothing but misery; heaven is the place where
there is nothing but virtue and, therefore, nothing but
happiness. This world is a world in which there is sin and
virtue and, therefore, misery and happiness. Howbeit the
Bible traces all of the virtue of this world to the mediation
of Christ and not to mere men themselves directly.

The religious sanctions against not loving God in the
heart cannot be imposed by man. By whom can they be
imposed? By whom other than God Himself, who reads
the heart and knows the inmost thoughts and intents of
the mind? who judges not after appearances. "The Lord
said unto Samuel, Look not on his countenance, or on the

height of his stature; because I have refused him: for the Lord seeth not as man seeth; for man looketh on the outward appearance, but the Lord looketh on the heart," 1 Samuel 16:7. "And before him shall be gathered all nations: and he shall separate them one from another, as a shepherd divideth his sheep from the goats: And he shall set the sheep on his right hand, but the goats on the left. Then shall the King say unto them on his right hand, Come, ye blessed of my Father, inherit the kingdom prepared for you from before the foundation of the world: For I was an hungered, and ye gave me meat: I was thirsty, and ye gave me drink: I was a stranger and ye took me in . . . Verily I say unto you, inasmuch as ye have done it unto one of the least of these my brethren, ye have done it unto me. Then shall he say also unto them on the left hand, Depart from me, ye cursed, into everlasting fire, prepared for the devil and his angels . . . Verily I say unto you, Inasmuch as ye did it not to one of the least of these, ye did it not to me," Matthew 25:32-35, 41-42, 45. "Every plant, which my heavenly Father hath not planted, shall be rooted up . . . Those things which proceed out of the mouth come forth from the heart; and they defile the man. For out of the heart proceed evil thoughts, murders, adulteries, fornications, thefts, false witness, blasphemies: These are the things which defile a man," Matthew 15:13, 18-20. "Thou hast set our iniquities before Thee, our secret sins in the light of Thy countenance," Psalm 90:8. "And thou, Solomon my son, know thou the God of thy father, and serve Him with a perfect heart and with a willing mind: for the Lord searcheth all hearts, and understandeth all the imaginations of the thoughts: if thou seek Him, He will be found of thee; but if thou forsake Him, He will cast thee off for ever," 1

Chronicles 23:9.

Another sanction which God imposes on the impeni-
tent is a tormented conscience. "The way of the transgres-
sors is hard," Proverbs 13:15. There is no rest for the
wicked. "The wicked flee when no man pursueth,"
Proverbs 28:1. The wrath of God abides on unbelievers.
"The Father loveth the Son, and hath given all things
into His hand. He that believeth on the Son hath everlasting life: and he that believeth not the Son shall not see
life; but the wrath of God abideth on him," John 3:35-36.
"Forasmuch then as the children are partakers of flesh
and blood, he also himself likewise took part of the same;
that through death he might destroy him that had the
power of death, that is, the devil; And deliver them who
through fear of death were all their lifetime subject to
bondage," Hebrews 2:14-15. "Thou rulest the raging of
the sea; when the waves thereof arise, Thou stillest them,"
Psalm 89:9.

As we have already observed, conscience is con-
scientia of that which goes along with knowledge. When
the mind sees something to be right, conscience
constrains the person to do it, and when the mind sees
something to be wrong conscience constrains the person
to eschew it. If this conscience is disobeyed it causes
inner pain. These compunctions or pricks of conscience
are so many inner lacerations which make their victim
miserable. Nothing external can serve as an ointment.
Pangs of conscience hurt regardless of the comfort of the
body. As we have seen, conscience makes even the
comforts of the body uncomfortable. It is either excusing
or accusing all the time, and when it is accusing it is
difficult to live with conscience. Many have been known
to take their lives, wrongly thinking they may thereby

escape their inward tormentor.

There seems to be only one way of finding any relief, besides doing what the conscience wants, and that is by moral anethesia. That is, the conscience may be desensitivized by keeping the mind preoccupied with other matters—perhaps with other and more terrible sins. So long as the mind is occupied with them, for so long it may be able to ignore the torments of conscience. This is the expulsive power of a new though false affection. This seems to be what the Bible means by "searing" the conscience. Conscience, like the body, may become too callous any longer to feel pain.

Another sanction which is closely related to conscience—but not identical—is a kind of intellectual restlessness. The great questions are not answered apart from God. One philosopher, when asked who he thought he was, replied that he wished he knew. Another thinker said that we must build upon the foundation of complete and unyielding despair. Still another said that, since there is no God, there is no purpose and no love in the universe. Human sciences can tell us some interesting things about the bodies and the worlds in which we live, but where we or they come from or are going these sciences cannot say. At the same time, the mind continues its search for the answers which it can never find apart from God. All the while it is hounded by the possibility that this God is quite discoverable, and only the mind's perversity prevents the discovery. Nor can it ever be sure that there will not be some dreadful punishment for this blindness. Thus its restlessness ever feeds upon itself.

The fourth sanction designed to prevent violations of the law of God is the judgment of the next world. First, this sanction catches up all the preceding and transcends

them. Thus it includes all the calamities of this world in
perfect measure of intensity and without cessation.
Second, it continues the torments of conscience, only
without any alleviation or possibility of preoccupation or
searing in any way open to its victim. The conscience is
still alive and fully sensitive, and the vision of the nature
of sin which activates it is perfectly clear. Third, the
intellectual uneasiness is utterly confirmed. The
misgiving which the mind had in this world is realized and
the mind knows total distress for total error. All the
inequities of the present life, all of common grace which
may exist here, all the defects of sensitivity which now
diminish the experience of the wrath of God shall there
disappear and there will be nothing but punishment and
grief in perfect degree and endless duration. This is what
the Bible calls hell. It is the place where the fire is not
quenched and the worm dieth not, Mark 9:44-46, where
God is known as a consuming fire, Hebrews 12:29, the
place prepared for the devils and his angels, Matthew
25:41, the place where "the angel swing his sickle on the
earth, and gathered the vintage of the earth, and threw it
into the great wine press of the wrath of God. . . ."
Revelation 14:19.

Let us return to the man who is not interested in repentance; to the man who has no disposition to repent
when he is commanded to do so; to the man who cannot
repent although he ought to do so. What does he do
when confronted by these sanctions? Does he repent, because failure to do so is visited with such terrible punishments? No, he is still not disposed to repent. It makes
no difference how great the punishment for impenitence
may be—if he does not have it in his heart to repent he
cannot repent. He could, under fear, pretend to repent,

but what would be the use? There is no deceiving God who knows the inmost thought. Just what would a man in that situation do? What could he do? Of course, he may pretend to believe that all this is all nonsense. There is no God; there is no more moral law; there is no punishment for law-breaking. But if he will think about these things, he will know that his contentions are untrue and will only aggravate his misery. Then he may put these things out of his mind. He will forget about them. But how can he forget them? How does a person forget that he is sitting over the furnace of hell? If he ever does forget about hell, that only guarantees that he will sometime fall into it. Forgetting is the most hopeless thing conceivable. It is the last thing which an awakened person will do. He must think about it. But when he things about it, the old sense of futility overwhelms him. What good is it to think of it? He cannot, he will not, he has no desire, no inclination to repent. But if he does not repent . . . .

Thus the person cannot continue as he is, happy, but neither can he do what he should do. There is only one other alternative, and that is to turn to God to beseech Him for the heart which the sinner needs. The Bible indicates that God is able to take away the heart of stone and give a heart of flesh; to make dead bones to live; to make a person a new creature. This miserable man may know that God is able to deliver him from these dread sanctions. So he may look to this God for help, although he does not love Him at all. At this moment, the man loves only himself. Still he is exposed to danger, and self-interest advises him to seek help from the God he does not love but hates. Indeed, he is looking to this God to change his heart so that he will love the God he now hates. This the man is desiring, not because he loves God but because he loves

himself. If God deals with the suppliant after his selfish
and hateful spirit there is no hope, but the man is hoping
that God will be constrained by His own mercy to have
pity. This he has good reason for hoping. This desperate,
sinful seeking of God is what the divine sanctions are designed to produce in the hearts of lost men.

Chapter 3

The Two Sources of Moral Laws

Cannibals often think that their peculiar rites have the sanction of the deity or deities. The vast majority of mankind does not agree with this judgment. Why not? Why does it make the opposite judgment, that God does not command any such thing? And there is the still more basic question: How do we know what God would or would not command, and what He has or has not commanded? In other words, what is the relation between revelation and ethics?

First of all, we note that when we speak of natural ethics, or the ethics of nature, what we mean is the ethics of natural revelation. That is, since we believe God to be the author of nature, we believe that ethics which is revealed by the course and constitution of nature to be the ethics revealed by God, the author of the course and constitution of nature. We do not attempt in this volume to prove the existence of God and the fact of His creatorship. We refer the reader to the companion volume to this one, *Reasons for Faith* (Soli Deo Gloria, 1995), chapters 3–6, for our argument in that area. Here we assume the existence of God and His authorship of the universe, and therefore that its laws are His laws. The question before us is this: Can God, and if so how does He, reveal, supernaturally, further moral obligations or obligations that even contravene the laws of nature?

We cannot deny that God could reveal further moral laws in a supernatural way. If God is God, the author and maintainer of the world, it surely lies within His power to issue further directives to His world, does it not? We cannot say to the cannibal, for example, that his notion that God commands cannibalism is impossible because God could make no such special communication. We cannot say that this tradition is false simply because there is no possibility of supernatural revelation. No, would we not have to admit this claim to the forum of our deliberation? And the same would have to go for any other claimed supernatural revelation; it could not be dismissed *a priori*. It would, on the contrary, have to be admitted *a priori*, on the supposition that it is not inherently impossible, and await a weighing of the evidence for and against its actuality. Likewise, if Abraham claimed that God commanded him to slay his own son, we cannot dismiss this on the ground that it is inconceivable that God revealed Himself to Abraham. No man knows enough to say that God could not reveal Himself and, therefore, that Abraham was necessarily mistaken. The possibility of revelation being admitted—nothing more than the possibility, but nothing less either—the evidence for the factuality of what is claimed must then be weighed.

If it is granted that God may Himself reveal new moral obligations, the question to be faced is how such a revelation would be recognized, and how false pretensions to revelation would be exposed as such. If such a claimed revelation appeared, would it not have to be consistent with what had already been revealed in nature? Suppose we say, "No, the author of nature must be permitted to change his mind if He sees fit to do so." But how can He see fit to change His mind if He knows all things from the beginning and there is no such thing as new information which could lead to a reevaluation of the situation and alteration of the commands concerning it? Or, since He is incapable of making a mistake because He does know all things perfectly, how can He wish to change His mind in order to correct anything? And, if He has no need to change His mind because of new information or a previous mistake, what other reason could there be for an apparent change of mind?

Perhaps the circumstances have changed, and commands which applied to one situation are changed now because the situation has changed. That is admittedly possible, that is, that God could change (not His mind, but) His commands if the situation to which they were addressed were changed. The question then is, has the human situation changed? Are humans not still male and female, married and given in marriage? Has the basic economy of human life been altered? No one claims that it has been. If not, who can say that there is any ground for a change of command? And if there is no ground for a change of command, must not all claimed revelations be consistent with what has already been given? It would seem so.

President James McCosh of Princeton University (from 1858 to 1888), heard, the dubious legend has it, some students in their dormitory room behaving in a rowdy manner. He went to their door to quiet them. When he knocked on the door they asked who it was. He is reported to have answered, "It's me, President McCosh." "Go away," they replied, "President McCosh would never say, 'It's me.' " (They presumed a man as well-educated as he would have said "It's I.")

In the same way, suppose that someone said he had

received a revelation from God telling men that it was their duty to tell lies. Would men not be justified in saying, "Go away, God would never command us to tell lies. It is inconsistent with His own character and His previous revelation in nature"?

The Mormon prophet, Joseph Smith, claimed that God had revealed to him that polygamy was permitted. Should Smith not have refused such a supposed communication as incompatible with the revelation of the Bible, which Smith professed to believe was God's? A man stabbed a prison chaplain and claimed later he heard a voice telling him to do it. Should he not have repudiated that as a divine communication inasmuch as God forbids the taking of a life except for crimes?

Every sharp observer will have smelled a rat in that last statement. "Is it not possible," he will ask, "that God knows of a crime which the chaplain committed but that no man knows of, and could by special revelation direct someone to take action so as to carry out just punishment?" Can anyone deny that God would know of crimes which people have committed but which have escaped detection and punishment? Hardly. What then? Since God does have such knowledge, how can we deny this revelation?

There is a difference between this claim and Joseph Smith's just mentioned. In that, God changes His mind. Such is not the case here. God does not change His mind. He may simply have revealed His knowledge and acted justly in accordance with it. His procedure would be different from what it had been, but it would not be inconsistent, so far as we have gone. He would not be saying in the Bible that crime should not be punished and in this revelation that it should be punished. He would simply be carrying out His declared policy of punishing crime, but doing it by means of a specially appointed rather than by a regularly elected officer. Would not that person be rash who would say God could not do that?

Well, then, how do we know that God did not reveal the death sentence to this man? The best answer to the question is, how do we know that He *did*? If a man claims that God is reversing His usual procedure of enforcing law through the powers that be, we will not deny, of course, that God can do that, but we must have proof that He has done so. We need this proof for several reasons.

First, if God does not authenticate such communications, what protection could there be against fanaticism and fraud? If no criteria of revelation were necessary, what distinction would there be between the mad dreams of Hitler and the seraphic enlightenment of Isaiah? Everyone, whether he be sane or mad, good or bad, could, without authentication, make the most fantastic claims in the name of God and command docile obedience.

Second, the resultant confusion, if such communications took place, would be inconsistent with the decency and order of nature. This is a universe in which laws hold sway; but unlimited claims to special communication from God would leave the highest part of the created universe as we know it—namely, man—with no settled order or authority. God's revelations could be claimed at random by anyone who chose to do so. This would make God himself the author of confusion, and if he were the author of confusion, then the very order of the universe would itself become confusing.

Third, men are so constituted that they can believe nothing without some measure of evidence. "Why" and "How" and similar questions are native to man. He never does anything or believes anything without some reason. The fact that some other man merely said so is not necessarily a reason, and "he said so" cannot be accepted on its own authority without some reason for so doing.

Someone will ask about the case of Abraham, commanded by God to sacrifice his son Isaac (Genesis 22:2). What of that? There are some differences between the claim that God told Abraham to kill his son and the claim that God told that man in prison to kill the chaplain. First, let it be remembered, as we have already observed, that there was nothing necessarily immoral in either command. God holds the right to the lives of all his creatures, and there could be no ground for denying that God may have known some reason why they should die in these instances. The problem is located elsewhere; namely, would God deviate from his rule of executing judgment upon men only by acts of nature and through duly constituted government? In the case of the unnamed man we found no reason to justify this deviation. Is the same true in Abraham's case?

Our second observation is that Abraham had already satisfied himself that he had been designated as an agent of revelation. This was not the first and only disclosure of God's will to this man. Already God had called him out of Ur of the Chaldees; of that he was persuaded. He knew, therefore, that God had made him a vehicle of revelation far beyond common human privilege. In His earlier disclosure to Abraham, God had not created a moral crisis, but merely a venturesome test of Abraham's faith. In the present test God is more exacting, but Abraham was already conditioned to receive revelation from God. Since it was possible that God had good and sufficient reason for taking Isaac's life which no father could deny, Abraham (assuming the request came from God, as he had reason to believe that it did) could not reasonably and morally disobey.

Third, there is in the case of Abraham a manifest testing. What tie could be closer than between a father and a son, especially between a father and the long-awaited son of his old age, who was, furthermore, the son of promise? If men must hate their children in order to be worthy of following the Son of God (Matthew 10:37), what more suitable test of Abraham's worthiness to be a disciple than just this? No such factor as this obtains in the other instance. The man simply claims a revelation to kill someone to whom he has no relation or tie. There is no strain on his affection, no testing of ultimate loyalty. But in Abraham's case there was. Nor can we doubt that Abraham realized it and understood the purpose of the trial.

Fourth, the patriarchal period was a time of special revelation. We cannot go into the argument for this point here, although we may refer to the companion volume *Reasons for Faith,* chapters 8 and 9, which deals with such matters. But the Bible does present a case for its inspiration and its continuing authentic revelation. Thus Abraham has been authenticated by none other than Jesus Christ, who, the evidence shows, is the very Son of God. According to the Bible itself, the period of revelation which occurred during Bible times has since ceased. So Abraham's case is believable from this viewpoint also, just as the other case is contradicted by this viewpoint.

Our first principle, then, for ascertaining whether a claim to revealed ethic is true is that it must not contradict the law of nature. This is the same as to say that special revelation must not contradict natural revelation, or that God must not contradict God. If He did contradict Himself, one revelation would reject the other and no revelation would be left standing. We are, therefore, on solid ground in saying that nothing can be an ethical principle of special revelation which is contrary to ethical principles of natural revelation.

This is the point at which to indicate that the above statement is by no means the same as saying that there can be no principle in special revelation that is *not contained* in natural revelation. There may very well be some specific duties given in special revelation that do not appear in natural revelation. God may be incapable of changing His mind, as we have shown, but does that imply that He is incapable of adding to the revelation of His mind? Apparently not.

Let us revert to Abraham. There would seem to be nothing in the nature of things that would make it impossible for God to reveal to Abraham that he should go to a land God would show him. Now there is no natural law that says a man should leave his present dwelling and migrate elsewhere, and surely there is nothing in nature to tell such a man where to migrate. If God commands Abraham to go elsewhere this is a new command, but one that does no violence to natural law. Indeed, it does not even become a positive law. That is, it applies to no one but Abraham. Followers of Abraham's faith, for example, have no obligation to emulate their ancestor in migration, and surely they need not start at Ur and from thence proceed to Canaan. Nevertheless, this was a duty for Abraham, and it was an item beyond the content of natural law.

Since this command was not contrary to natural law, it needed only some evidence of its sanction in order to become binding on the person to whom it was given. If a command were truly contrary to natural law, no amount of presumed evidence could be found, for God could not contradict Himself. If God contradicted Himself, He would not be God. But since no such problem arises here, the person to whom the presumed command is addressed need concern himself solely with the evidence for its divine source.

It is worth observing here that even such a command as we are now considering ultimately rests on a great ethical principle of natural law. That principle is that the creature should be obedient to the Creator. All men recognize, probably intuitively, that they owe allegiance to the one to whom they owe their existence. This principle is in play here, although only tacitly and implicitly. That is, Abraham recognized his obligation to obey God. He needed only to be convinced that it was God who had spoken.

Granted that a positive command of revelation may have sanction for a particular individual (as for Abraham in the example), how can we know when a supernaturally revealed law carries an obligation for mankind generally? The answer seems to be simple: If it is addressed to mankind generally. How does Abraham know that a command has application to him? By its being addressed to him. How does the world know that a command addressed to Abraham alone does not apply to us? Because it is not addressed to us. How do we know a command does apply to us? By its being addressed to us. It is that simple in principle, though it may not be as simple in practice to ascertain whether a particular command is addressed to mankind in general.

Some of the commands given at Sinai were simply and

solely addressed to Israel and its proselytes. Certain cere-
monial regulations and temple procedures, and the like,
were given with meticulous precision, and the people of
God were commanded to observe them with the same ex-
actness and were regarded as culpable if they did not do
so. These regulations were never made universal, except
the Ten Commandments or moral law. But the
Decalogue's universally binding nature was not because
it was given to the Jews at Sinai; it was universally binding because it was given to Gentiles also, being written on
their hearts and consciences.

If we suppose that the Bible contains supernaturally
revealed moral laws, let us compare these with naturally
revealed moral laws. To be more specific, let us select some
moral laws of Christ from the Bible and compare them
with natural laws.

An *a priori* observation may be in order. There cannot be any conflict between the law of Christ and the law
of conscience if Christ is a divine person. If Christ is divine, as we have attempted to show elsewhere (*Reasons for
Faith*, chapter 9), He would not contradict Himself and
therefore could not say opposite things in the hearts of
men and through His own mouth while on earth, could
He? He would no more contradict Himself in these two areas than He would contradict Himself in the different
Testaments. So we may deduce, without investigation,
that if our previous argument that Christ is the Son of
God is true, and if the law of noncontradiction is true,
then the law of nature and the law of Christ will not contradict each other but repeat or complement each other.

Christ does not repudiate the sixth commandment. He
points out what is involved in the law of murder in addition to overt murder, but He does not deny that murder

in the overt expression is wrong (Matthew 5:21–26). So in this area He is manifestly in agreement with what nature teaches. We have noticed in our discussion of cannibalism that man by nature knows it is wrong to take the life of other human beings without adequate reason. This Christ confirms to be true.

When Christ goes on to observe that the spirit of murder (which may not express itself in an overt act) is murder, does he leave nature behind? Is he here penetrating a veil where nature could not? Does nature stop with a condemnation of literal killing but know nothing of a sin of hate that stops short of actual murder? Does man as a moral being, to put the matter another way, think there is nothing wrong with hating other persons? Does man's conscience make it possible for him to be at ease although he is full of hatred, so long as he restrains this hate from boiling over into assault?

It seems to us that to ask such questions is to answer them. No man will say that it is morally right to hate a person without cause. Does not every man have a conviction of guilt when he does not give a fellow his true recognition as a fellow human? Christ's teaching strikes a chord in the human heart, does it not?

Such questions, however, are merely an appeal to empirical experience. There is a profounder and more important question. Does nature actually teach such doctrine? Does natural law make clear that we should not hate, for example?

Suppose we begin our investigation of this point with a familiar bit of verse:

I do not like thee, Dr. Fell,
The reason why I cannot tell.
But this one thing I know full well,
I do not like thee, Dr. Fell.

The poem seems at first glance to justify an arbitrary dislike. But on second glance there are at least two reasons
embodied in the doggerel which argue otherwise. First,
the poem is funny. It is meant to be a joke, and it evokes
amusement. Now if this arbitrary dislike were considered
a perfectly normal human feeling, it would not seem
funny, would it?

Second, "the reason why I cannot tell" is not a denial
of a reason, but a denial that the person understands it
clearly. Rather, the line seems to imply, if we take this
humorous bit seriously, that there is a reason for this
feeling. In other words, the ditty is funny because it gives
no reasons for this behavior, but when it is taken seriously it really does assume that there is a reason after all.
This would mean, judging from this bit of ethical philosophy, that people do not consider it an inalienable right to
dislike other persons.

But why is it not right to hate another person? Why
may we not say: "I will hate whom I will. It is my hatred
and I can do with it what I want. No one is going to tell
me whom I can and cannot hate. I will hate whom I
choose?" Well, for one thing, this is the stuff of which
murder is made, and we have already seen that the law of
nature forbids murder. A person may hate without murdering, but he cannot murder without hating. Hating is
the necessary first step in the commission of the crime. As
a matter of fact, is it not evident that murder is nothing
but hate in action? Hating is wishing ill to a person, and

killing him is only the utmost expression of ill will a man can make. If a person harbors pure hatred toward another, it is clear that that person would commit murder unless something were restraining him. He has all that is necessary for him to commit murder, insofar as his inner disposition is concerned. Since, therefore, hate is of the essence of murder, and murder is clearly condemned by nature, we must say that hate is condemned by nature.

Second, hate, if it did not express itself in murder and thereby remove its object, would make the hater miserable. Hate wishes ill to another, and the ultimate ill is death. If hate is not to be satisfied by the death of its object, it will rage as a powerful frustration in the hater's soul. This will make him miserable. The fact that he may deserve to be miserable is not the point before us at the moment. The point is that hate is contrary to the law of nature because it makes the person who has that feeling miserable, if it does not make him an actual murderer. If, therefore, murder were in accord with nature, then nature and nature's God would be the author of evil and misery. To follow nature would make men, of all creatures, most miserable, and their very ability to think and be moral would be their greatest liability. This we know to be contrary to the structure and goal of nature.

This second point was theoretical: we argued that if men were frustrated they would be miserable. The third point parallels the preceding one, but on experiential rather than theoretical grounds. Not only can we state on logical grounds that if men were haters though not murderers they would be frustrated, and that if they were frustrated they would be miserable, but we can also say as a matter of personal testimony that hate is a feeling which makes the hater miserable. It is not a pleasant feeling.

Someone may demur at this point and say, "I am not sure about this. When I think that Hitler has been killed it makes me feel good. When I hear that some cruel sadist who has tortured children is to be punished for his inexcusable crimes, I feel good. On the other hand, when I know of someone who is committing crimes with impunity, I am distressed. When I hear him being praised I am still more distressed. I feel that he should get his just deserts, and his just deserts mean punishment or an ill fate. So I must confess that if this is hate, it does not make me feel bad but good. And moreover I find most people, indeed all, feel the same way."

We cannot quarrel with these feelings; in fact, we must admit that we have them too. But we do quarrel with them as evidences of hate. We would say that the clue to the nature of this feeling appears in the expression "just deserts." This feeling is a desire that men should receive what they deserve. This is not the same thing as wishing a person ill, although that man's just desert may bring him suffering. But we do not want ill to befall the man; we want him to receive his just deserts. We want any man to receive his just deserts, whether they bring good or ill. We do not want men to suffer ill or good, without reference to the person; we want the person to receive what he ought to receive.

This can hardly be called hate, because it is not a feeling of ill will toward a person. On the contrary, it is directed to justice and the upholding of the moral law. It wishes that justice be maintained, and therefore it desires that guilty persons be punished. Such a feeling is perfectly consistent with a hope that the guilty person might turn from his evil ways and thereby deserve not punishment but praise. Ill will or hate does not feel that way at all. It seeks ill for a particular person whether he deserves it or not. It is not rational or moral but blind and prejudiced.

We have attempted to show that Christ's law against hate is an implicit part of natural law. What about the other parts of Christ's exposition of the sixth commandment? He says that anyone who says to his brother "Raca" is in danger of the council (Matthew 5:22). This seems to mean that whoever slights his fellow man is guilty of the essence of murder. Whoever treats his neighbor with no respect or significance as a human being—who uses his neighbor for his own benefit—is a killer. In the words of Immanuel Kant's theory of ethics, such a man is treating his neighbor as a means rather than as an end. Does nature permit what Christ and other ethicists have forbidden? Or is this, too, a part of natural law?

Indeed it is, for this too has the potentiality of murder. If another human being is used merely as a means, it is immediately clear that should he be more "useful" dead than alive his murder is certain. Should he be inconveniently in the way, this man, who would not be considered at all if he were not in the way, will be removed from the path. If death is the most expeditious and satisfactory way of carrying out this removal, so be it. If he is not murdered it will be because some other factors, such as fear of the police, have come into play. But the feeling of regarding a fellow man as a means rather than as an end will not hold back the murderer's hand for a moment. We can see this without special revelation showing us. When Christ says it, we see but a revealed confirmation of what natural law already enjoins.

Does all this mean that there are no moral principles

revealed by special means that are not also revealed by natural means? If so, what purpose does special revelation have in this regard? The answer is that it is given for the purpose of confirming natural revelation. Also, natural revelation, insofar as it is related to special revelation, has been given to prepare people for special revelation. That is, naturally revealed moral principles are the principles by which we test the authenticity of special revelation. As we have seen, if the morality revealed specially were not consistent with that which is revealed naturally, we would be compelled to conclude that the special revelation was spurious.

How, if natural revelation can be used as a criterion for testing special revelation, could special revelation be considered a confirmation of natural revelation? Would it not be circular reasoning to say that we use naturally revealed morality to test specially revealed morality and then say that the latter may serve as confirmation of the former? If the natural authenticates the special, the special can hardly authenticate the natural as well.

So perhaps we had better rephrase the matter: specially revealed morality tends to elucidate and clarify natural morality. Before we are finished we may be able to show that in so doing it also provides a type of confirmation. But first let us note how specially revealed morality elucidates natural morality.

We said above that what Christ taught in the Sermon on the Mount was already revealed in the moral thought of mankind. But, if so, how can this special revelation be said to elucidate the natural revelation concerning hatred and murder? Clearly we can say this much: Christ's teaching elucidates the natural morality for most people. The vast majority of mankind do not think very much at all, and certainly not very deeply about the nature of morals. In their preoccupation with the routine of life, they do not stop for reflection. The result is that the laws written in the course and constitution of nature are read only by the few (generally, those who read books on ethics). Not thinking much about these things, the masses are not likely to remember or be guided by them. Furthermore, they are in a world which does not pay much attention to these pointers and which is guided largely by other principles.

Now special revelation is given so that he who runs may read. Who can know anything about Christ, for example, and ever forget that hatred is considered a moral evil? Probably there is not one person enlightened by the natural moral law for every thousand who are enlightened by the law of Christ. So we may say that special revelation calls attention, makes an indelible impression, and imposes with an immediate divine sanction the nature and obligations of morality—natural morality.

Revealed morality does more than that. Not only do most people not think about the natural moral laws, and surely not of their more advanced and difficult principles, but when they do think of them they tend to think very superficially. Their hearts do not dispose them toward morals and holiness, as both Kant and the Bible would say. At this point also, specially revealed ethics makes an essential contribution. It shows plainly and unmistakably not only that there is a moral law, but what lies in its profound inner meaning.

In this process of illuminating the obscured lines of moral law, revealed law is both confirming and confirmed by natural law. Each tells the same story. One may tell it more plainly than the other, but they agree on what they tell. When nature speaks, we say that this is the voice of revelation; when revelation speaks, we say that this is the voice of nature.

So we have seen that, if revelation morality is to be trusted, it must not violate the morality of nature, and furthermore it must be consistent with and confirmed by it. Granted that this is so, let us suppose that the revealed morality includes some things not contained in the revelation from nature. We have already mentioned the command to Abraham to go into a land the Lord would show him. This we said was for Abraham only, because it was addressed to him and to him only. For any such positive command to be an obligation for others, we said, it must be addressed to others. The question now is: Do we know that we now have revelation and therefore can trust that whatever it says to mankind in general should be obeyed? Is the fact that this claimed special revelation includes a moral content, consistent with and confirmed by natural law, proof that those portions that go beyond natural law—what is not necessarily consistent with or confirmed by natural law—is also to be obeyed? After all, one does not need supernatural knowledge to state an ethic that is identical with the natural law; any discerning person, without supernatural aid, would be able to determine and disclose such ethics, and some persons have, as a matter of fact, done so. Therefore, how do we know that we have revelation simply because a claimed revelation contains morality consistent with and confirmed by nature?

The answer is that we do not. But if we do not know that we have revelation, then why should we obey what it says beyond that contained also in natural law? Answer: we should not, unless we get proof that this is revelation. As yet we do not have this.

All we have done so far is to indicate what a claimed revelation must show in order not to be rejected! We have not told what is necessary if it is to be accepted. Of course, its consistency with nature counts in its favor, just as truly as the absence of such consistency would disqualify it. But what more is necessary?

For one thing, in order to be revelation it must claim revelation. We have assumed all along that we are dealing with a claimed revelation, but now we are insisting on this point. If a communication came from God, we have every reason to believe that God would make its origin clear—that He would say this was God speaking. While revelations may claim to be from God which are not, we cannot imagine that a revelation really from God would not identify itself as from God.

Furthermore, this claim must be supported by some evidence of a positive character. Anyone can say he speaks with God's authority; he could be a liar, but still intelligent enough to say only things consistent with natural revelation. Admittedly this would be difficult for a pretender, but not impossible. So we need more than a mere claim plus the absence of inconsistencies in order to prove the presence of God or his messenger. Would there not also need to be some indication that only God could give to prove that God was present?

So long as man could make bold and unscrupulous claims, if God were to reveal Himself He would be obliged to do more than this. He would be obliged to do or say something that only He could do or say. In other words, for a claimed revelation to be accepted as authentic there must be supernatural words and/or supernatural works. What are these supernatural works but fulfilled prophecy and other miracles? Again, it is not our purpose here to

show that the Bible possesses these indicia. We have attempted to do that in the companion volume to this one.
But we can note here that the best authentication of all
would be a supernatural person. In Jesus Christ we have
just such a supernatural person. He is the revelation,
gives the revelation, and certifies the revelation of sacred
Scripture.

If this is so, then we are ready to face the question,
what should we do about duties over and above natural
law which are revealed in this special revelation (if there
are such duties)? Are we to reject them as something not
revealed by nature? Hardly. It would be rash to tell God
that since He had not said something in nature He is not
allowed to say it in revelation. This would be an instance
of the creature dictating to the Creator, and that could
hardly be considered sane, let alone ethical behavior.

On the contrary, the rational and the moral thing
would be to say, in the words of Samuel when he was
convinced the voice of God was speaking, "Speak, Lord,
for thy servant heareth" (I Samuel 3:9). This seems to us
so evident that nothing more need be said about it. The
hard point in this discussion is not deciding what to do
when God tells us what to do, but how to decide when
God has told us what to do. If that has been settled—that
God has spoken in the Bible—our only remaining question will be to determine what He has said.

In a certain sense, all duties that are incumbent on
Christians are also duties for non-Christians as well. That
is, since all unconverted persons have the duty of being
converted and are to be blamed if they do not fulfill that
obligation (their own inability being no excuse, but only
an aggravation of their guilt), they have the duties which
follow on conversion. To be sure, they should not take

the Lord's Supper while unconverted, but nonetheless they are to blame for not being converted and taking the Lord's Supper. This is one step removed, but it is still part of the moral picture. Unbelievers are to blame for not taking the Lord's Supper because they are to blame for not putting themselves in a position where they could take the Lord's Supper.

Bearing this in mind, we may address ourselves to the question, what are Christian or biblical ethics in distinction from natural ethics? Just as there are a natural theology and a revealed theology, so there would seem to be a natural and a revealed morality. But just as the natural theology is included in revealed theology, so the natural morality is included in the revealed ethics. But at the same time, in this volume, we are treating revealed or Christian ethics proper—those ethical principles contained in Christianity that are not contained in natural ethics.

In the next part of this volume (chapters 4–13) we will discuss the fundamental structure of morals and the duties revealed in natural law. We will then (chapters 14–20) consider those duties that are revealed only in Scripture, remembering that Scripture also reveals duties that have been revealed in nature as well.

Part 2

Naturally Revealed
Moral Laws

Chapter 4

The First Commandment

"Thou shalt have no other gods before me" (Exodus 20:2).

Should ethics ever be negative? That is, should there be don'ts as well as do's? Or should we eliminate the negative and accentuate the positive? To forbid or not to forbid, that is the moral question.

To illustrate how far the eliminate-the-negative approach has influenced modern thought, let me relate an amateur experiment we once conducted. Speaking to a group of high-school students, I asked them to answer a question spontaneously, saying the first thing that came to their minds without thinking or deliberating. Once they agreed to answer immediately and in unison, I then posed this question: "The Ten Commandments—are they predominantly positive or negative?" (We had previously explained the meaning of the terms "positive" and "negative.") The answer came immediately in a resounding chorus: "Positive."

Now there are actually only two positive commands in the decalogue: "Remember the Sabbath day to keep it holy" and "Honor thy father and mother." The other eight are all "Thou shalt not's." The beginning and the ending commandments are negative. All these students had heard the Ten Commandments, known them, and in some cases they had memorized them. But they thought of the com-

45

mandments as positive in tone. No one could get that impression from the commandments themselves. There seems to be no other explanation than that the emphasis on positives is so much in the air that youths assume the commandments are of such a nature.

Another amateur experiment seems to have shown the same thing. We have asked many high-school youth groups what was the most common ethical teaching of Christ. We stress the fact that we are asking for the teaching he stated most, reiterated most, insisted on most. Only once in many tries have we found a young person who has given the correct answer. As a matter of fact, most of the time they are not even "warm," as we would say in a certain game. They are not in the right area. They invariably mention such maxims as "love your enemies," "go the second mile," "turn the other cheek," "do good," "forgive seven times seventy times," the Golden Rule, and the like—all of them positive injunctions. Almost never do they mention a negative teaching. But Henry Joel Cadbury indicates that the ethical teaching on which Christ placed most emphasis was a negative one, "deny thyself."

The Ten Commandments are not only largely negative, but they seem to be based on the assumption of human sinfulness. No optimistic view of human nature, as now prevails around us, underlies the Decalogue. Such a heavily negative code can only mean that its author thinks its subjects are prone to evil and need to be warned about succumbing to their natural tendencies. If men were seen as having no inclination to evil, it would be impossible to explain the strongly prohibitory character of these laws. Indeed, all laws are primarily negative in character. They are generally "thou shalt not's." When we think of law we think of some limitation, something that is taboo.

Actually the law is positive at heart. However negative the form of statement may be, the fulfillment of the law requires a positive disposition. As Paul says, love is the fulfilling of the law (Romans 13:10). Law itself may forbid the expression of some evil disposition, but actually to prevent such an expression one must have a positive respect and affection for the law. The absence of this feeling will make a person a hater, and usually a breaker, of the law.

Let us now consider the significant content of this first commandment. We find that a theological truth is placed as the fundamental principle of ethics. At the head of the commandments is the command to have no god but God. This statement is not placed first by chance; it is in this position because all commands must be kept with an eye on God—with respect to His will. It is quite possible to do the other things commanded of us, but with our eye on other gods. We may keep the Sabbath for business reasons; we may not murder for personal reasons; we may not steal for social reasons. To observe any of these commandments for any of these other reasons is the same as to have those reasons as our god, to worship the creature rather than the Creator.

It can be asked whether obedience for ulterior motives is not actually worse than disobedience. Which is better: to avoid murder because it is inconvenient, or to commit murder from hate? Obviously it is better to avoid murder, even if for no other reason than that it is inconvenient. But both of these alternatives assume a disregard for God. In such cases, whether we refrain from murder or commit it, our behavior has no respect to God, and is a violation of the first commandment. Avoiding murder only from reasons of convenience, thereby seeming to obey God while having no respect for Him, being hypocritical, is worse even than the act of murder.

The choice now is between an honest murderer and a dishonest nonmurderer. Which is worse? As far as God, who reads the heart, is concerned the latter is a double offender. While the former disregards God, the other does so as well and adds to that the hypocrisy of pretending to do otherwise. Would he not, therefore, be a greater sinner in God's eyes than the honest murderer?

But what of society? Obviously it would have been better for a murdered man had he run into a dishonest nonmurderer rather than an honest murderer. But it is not necessarily the same for society in general. If the hypocritical nonmurderer advocated hypocrisy as a way of life—if he maintained that outward observance of the law was alone necessary—and if this ethical heresy thereby spread to others, this would do to the others more damage than murder. They may abandon faith in God. Even loss of life is not as serious as the loss of God.

To summarize: this principle of respect to God is more important than all other commands because doing the other commands without this principle is of no real value to the person who does them, nor to society if the general welfare of society is considered.

This explains why Christ said that if any man "hate not his father, and mother, and wife, and children, and brethren, and sisters, yea, and his own life also, he cannot be my disciple" (Luke 14:26). Many interpreters suggest that this strong word really means not literally "hate" but "love less." There is some truth in that, but if the word "hate" can be misleading, so can the expression "love less" be equally misleading in the other direction. "Love less" conveys the comparative idea and suggests, in this context, that a disciple of Christ may love his father, etc., as he loves Christ but not as much. It gives the impression of a quantitative distinction: one may love both Christ and his father, but Christ, being the greater, must have a greater portion of our affection and our father, being the lesser, must have a lesser portion. But let us see if this exposition actually fits the teaching.

If Christ claimed a greater measure of the devotion of the human heart than man's nearest relatives were entitled to have, He must have thought himself to be more than a mere human being. For among human beings no one can have a greater right to a person's affection than his immediate family. Christ claimed this greater affection because He regarded Himself as divine and maintained that men owed Him the allegiance which belongs to God. This can explain, as nothing else could, how Christ could make such a claim on the hearts of men which demanded precedence above natural affection.

But if this is the explanation of Christ's claim for greater love than a person has for his nearest relatives, it actually lays claim to more than that. That is, if Christ must be divine in order to demand more affection than the nearest of family can claim, as a divine being He could lay claim to the whole heart as rightly belonging to Him alone. He would be the giver of friends and family, and the one who takes them away. He would be the source of filial affection and love of friends. He would be infinitely above them all. He therefore has a right to the whole human heart and no one else has any right to the heart except as He commands it. Thus, for example, the first commandment is "Thou shalt have no other gods before Me" and we get down to the fifth before there is mention of honoring fathers and mothers. And the fifth commandment is binding only because God commands it; if God had not commanded it, it would not be binding.

So we see that Christ and God command the heart of men entirely. There can be no other love but to them and to those whom they command us to love. The love for any human being, therefore, is not merely *quantitatively* less than that owed to the "Father of spirits," but it is *qualitatively* different. His love is unique and no other love can be compared to it. So, in a certain sense, to interpret the word "hate" as "love less" does great violence to Christ's intention. In comparison with love for God and His Son, all other love is nothing. It does not exist. If any other object should actually compete with the God of heaven for the affection of the human heart, the moral person must literally hate the idol. This would be no ignoble and sinful hate, but rather the perfect hatred of the Psalmist: "I hate them with perfect hatred: I count them mine enemies" (Psalm 139:22).

The commandments may be reduced to the love of God and the love of man, but the decalogue itself says nothing of love explicitly. Yet love is implicit in all the commandments, as we shall see. How is it implicit in this first and fundamental commandment? How does the command to have no other gods in the presence of God involve the love of God?

Positively speaking, the fulfillment of this first commandment requires love of God. How can we exclude all others from His presence unless we love Him? If, on the other hand, we do love Him, what room will there be for any other gods? We may love Him and have room for love for other beings, but not for other gods. Other gods are incompatible with Him; other beings are not. If we love other beings for His sake, because they are His creatures and because He desires us to love them, we are not making them competitors with our devotion to Him but, on the contrary, expressions of it. But if we love them as gods, as beings demanding our worship and devotion, we deny Him, for He is the infinite God who has sole crown rights over us. If we give any other being any right over us, however small, we are therein denying God; that is, we are denying Him as God, denying that He has the sole authority which He claims. If, therefore, we love any other beings as gods, we do not love Him as God, and if we do love Him as God then there is no room for any others as gods.

This is the meaning of Christ's words: "No man can serve two masters: for either he will hate the one, and love the other; or else he will hold to the one, and despise the other. Ye cannot serve God and mammon" (Matthew 6:24). This is immediately clear with respect for claimants for absolute sway over the heart. There can be nothing but constant friction between two such contestants, and the heart thus divided would be in hopeless inner conflict. But it is not quite as immediately clear why a master such as God and a master which claimed only partial allegiance would be in conflict. That is, suppose a person wished to do what he wished to do, without reference to anything or anybody else, only once in a while. Suppose, for example, that he had one of those cursing trees in his backyard, to which he would permit himself to go and swear only when the pressures became too much to endure. Suppose he was perfectly willing to obey the commands, generally speaking, and demanded only the right to lose his patience and profane all that is holy once in a great while, when he simply could not suppress the desire any longer. Why would such moderate immorality cause him to hate God? He denies that he does. He asserts that he loves God 99 percent of the time and gives way to disobedience on only very rare occasions. Surely that could not be considered unreasonable, he asks, and certainly it could not be called hating God, could it?

Yes, it could. Yes, it must. Why? For this reason: God requires 100 percent obedience. He tolerates no other gods, part-time or otherwise. That is the nature of God. He demands total surrender to Him, and to Him alone. This means that if a person wants even partial sovereignty over his own life to do what he pleases and to serve what he will, he must necessarily resent such a being as God. He will complain that God is too monopolistic, too exclusive, too jealous. (Indeed God calls Himself a jealous God.) This God will be considered too vain: He wants all glory for Himself. He is too self-centered: everything must revolve around Him. This will be too much for any person who wishes to retain some liberty, to have some area of thought and behavior which he may call his own and no one else's. He must either give up such notions or resent the living God. There is no other alternative. He must love the one and hate the other (gods), or love the gods and hate God.

Christ, in His summary of the moral law, makes the second part, the love of neighbor, derivative from the first part, love of God. He said, "Ye have heard that it hath been said, Thou shalt love thy neighbor, and hate thine enemy. But I say unto you, Love your enemies, bless them that curse you, do good to them that hate you, and pray for them which despitefully use you, and persecute you; That ye may be the children of your Father which is

in heaven; for He maketh His sun to rise on the evil and
on the good, and sendeth rain on the just and the unjust"
(Matthew 5:43–45). Love for man is derivative from love
for God in several ways.

First, and most obviously, it is derived from the commandment of God. We love whom our Creator commands
us to love. If He commanded us to love the devil, as He
does command us to love devilish men, we should do so.
At the same time, if He commanded us, even under normal
circumstances, to hate our dearest friends we should do
so. He is God, and we must have no other gods in His
presence.

A second way in which our love for men is derivative
from our love for God is in its source. That is, we love because He first loved us. He not only teaches us that we
should love our fellow men, but He inclines our hearts
that way. If there is any genuine love from man to man, it
comes from the heart of God. True love is born of the
Spirit of God, and men love when the Spirit of God is
shed abroad in their hearts.

Third, there is no possibility of any separation
between the two. That is to say, if there is true love for
God, there must necessarily be love for man; and
conversely, if there is true love for man, there must be
true love for God. The man who is not charitable to his
fellow man does not love God, and the man who does not
worship God is not charitable toward his fellow man even
though he may give him charity.

Let us illustrate. If a man is hungry and destitute
through no fault of his own (as distinguished from a professional bum who may be hungry and destitute not because he could not earn, but because he would not, as far
as any effort other than begging is concerned, be

otherwise), and you, although able to help him, refuse to do so, you do not love God. God commands us to love one another, to bear one another's burdens, and to do good, as He himself does. Our refusal to help this needy suppliant is, therefore, a refusal to obey God.

On the other hand, if we refuse to read God's Word and worship in His house, we do not love our fellow men. Why is this so? Because by disobeying God we are certain to bring judgment on ourselves which shall inevitably have a bad effect on others also, especially those closest to us. Our very example, if followed by others, would lead them to the same judgment, which is the worst disaster which we could bring upon them. We do not, therefore, love men unless we love God, any more than we love God unless we love men.

Chapter 5

The Second Commandment

"Thou shalt not make unto thee any graven image, or any likeness of any thing that is in heaven above, or that is in the earth beneath, or that is in the water under the earth: Thou shalt not bow down thyself to them, nor serve them: for I the Lord thy God am a jealous God, visiting the iniquity of the fathers upon the children unto the third and fourth generation of them that hate me; And shewing mercy unto thousands of them that love me, and keep my commandments" (Exodus 20:4–6).

This second commandment exhibits a significant addition to the content of the first. The first commandment defines the object of worship, the second the method of worship. Commandment number one tells Who alone may be the object of our worship; commandment number two shows how He is to be worshiped.

There is an obligation to worship God, but no less an obligation to worship Him in a certain manner. It is important that God be worshiped, but also a matter of duty that He be worshiped correctly. For example, if we attempted to worship God by sacrificing our children to Him, this method of worship would soon remove all potential worshipers.

Implicit in this command is the notion that the method by which God is to be worshiped is determined by Him. That is to say, it is part of the moral law, natural and revealed, how God is to be worshiped, and the matter is not left to individual choice. Free worship, therefore, must mean freedom to follow God's laws of worship, not man's. Indeed there can be no meaning in free worship except freedom to worship as God commands. We must be free of men so that we may be free to be constrained by God.

What is the form of worship forbidden in the second commandment? Note that there is no forbidding the use of visual images as such. The prohibition of visual images in worship is: "thou shalt not bow down to them nor serve them." This seems to mean that God does not want to be worshiped by means of intermediate objects to which gestures are directed. We do not say that He does not wish idols to be worshiped; this is already obvious from what has been forbidden in the first commandment. The second commandment is not a mere repetition of the first, but rather it has reference to something more than the wrong object of worship—namely, as we have already noted, the wrong method. The Israelites, to whom these ten commandments were given, professed to worship Jehovah. There was no question about that. What needed to be said was that they were to worship Him *only,* and *how* to worship Him only.

Indeed, there is a question whether, in one sense of the word, there is or ever was such a thing as idolatry. If idolatry is defined as the worship of material objects of some kind, would anyone plead guilty of the charge? Did any savage ever suppose that he was worshiping a block, a stone, a tree, a river, or a beetle? Apparently all animists considered these things merely cult objects, and their worship was directed to some invisible and intangible being or spirit which was somehow related to these objects, but not identified with them. Perhaps the spirit was thought to inhabit the object, pervade it, manifest himself by it, or appoint it as his representative. But did any primitive ever suppose that this piece of matter was a god before which he should actually bow and worship, and which controlled his destiny? Hardly.

If it is true that no one ever confused the being which was worshiped with the artifact used in its worship, how could the second commandment be supposed to forbid "idolatry"? On the other hand, if the second commandment does not mean to prohibit so-called idolatry, what did it intend but that Jehovah was not to be worshiped by idolatrous means? The worthiness of the divine object of worship was not to be accepted as an excuse for the unworthiness of the means by which He was worshiped. He had spoken on the matter, and there could be no misunderstanding: true worship must not be conducted in a false manner.

What is the general application of this principle that God Himself prescribes how He will be worshiped? Does this mean that no man should ever use anything in His worship of God which God has not specifically revealed? It would seem so, would it not?

It should not be surprising that God prescribes the method of His own worship. When a son gives his father a present at Christmas time, it is understood, to be sure, that he may give what he wishes, since he has no obligation to give anything. But, as a matter of fact, will he give what he wishes without reference to his father's desires? For example, he could, if he chose, give his father lipstick. That would be his privilege, you will admit. After all, he is giving the present voluntarily; he does not have to give anything. But still, unless he is joking, he will not give something that cannot be used. So he gives a tie.

Is that all to the matter? Hardly. Would he give his father a bow tie if father never wore bow ties? Not likely. What then is the controlling principle? He wants to give what his father wants—that is the controlling principle, even in gift-giving. Would it be otherwise with reference to God? Would we wish to give Him what He does not want? Would we not rather recognize the natural duty of giving to God what God wants? So, just as a son will try to ascertain what his father wants for Christmas in order to give a pleasing gift, so we will seek to ascertain what worship God desires. Of course, if this is true even in optional matters such as gift-giving, how much more is it applicable to matters of duty; and if it is true between man and man, how much more so between man and God?

It would be rather presumptuous, if not foolhardy, to give your father something which you knew he did not like and would not accept. Would it be less so to offer God what He has forbidden? But you may reply that it would not be thought of as presumptuous if you had thought your father wanted what you had given him, even if it turned out that he certainly did not. He would know that your heart was right. Why could God not recognize, in the case of "strange fire," that the worshipers meant well? This is not inconceivable. But suppose you made no effort to find out what your father wanted and proceeded out of a lazy indifference to give him what you thought, without studying the matter, he might want. Your father would not be happy, would he? Likewise, if God has revealed His will and men worship in other ways that those which are revealed, not having taken the care to ascertain what He has revealed, is it possible that their heart is in the right place? Can they plead sincere ignorance who have not taken the trouble to know the facts? Would their profession of ignorance be sincere?

If a person says, "I do not worship the image, but the being represented by it; I do not worship idols, but I worship God by means of idols"—what shall we say to that? Can we say that he who uses images is not in fact truly worshiping God thereby? Yes, we can, and for a very simple reason: because God says that He is not to be worshiped that way. God, after all, ought to know when He is being worshiped and when not. If He forbids worship in this mode, we conclude that He will not accept it. Even though the worshiper feels warm about the heart, or even claims an experience of God and a mystical assurance that God is pleased with this worship, we know that the person has not succeeded in worshiping God, for God has so revealed. What God says about worship is infinitely more significant than what the worshiper says about it. "If you love Me," Christ says, "keep My commandments." It will not do for us to say, "We love You, Lord, but we do not choose to keep Your commandments about worship. We will worship You, but in our own way." This is called in the Bible "will worship" and is distinguished from true worship of God.

How would men know from nature what type of worship God commands? Would they know enough from natural revelation not to worship God as a physical object? Yes, because they could know from nature that the God who made all things is an invisible spirit and not to be identified with tangible objects. As we have said, the most primitive people distinguish between their cult objects and the gods which they worship. They know that God is not to be identified with these objects. Would a man also know from nature that God was not to be worshiped *by means* of these? Granted that the primitive would know from nature the first commandment of the decalogue, would he also know the second? Would he know the way of worship as well as the object of worship? Could he reasonably be expected to know that he should not bow down to these cult objects? We think so, for several reasons.

First, men may know by natural revelation that if God is an infinite spirit, it would be dangerous, to say the least, to worship Him by means of physical objects. Man is a bodily being and, as such, is prone to think in terms of bodily desires and needs. It would be very easy, if God were worshiped by means of some physical object, to forget that God was not material also. There is something confining about such worship, and it is quite in contrast to the infinite character of God. To be sure, man is a finite being and his capacity to grasp the infinite is limited. But is this any reason to use cult objects that tend to suggest the limitation of God? Would it not be particularly easy for children, and for childish adults, quickly to associate God with this image? Has such confusion not resulted in persons of higher intelligence? If so, could it not easily take place with those of lower intelligence? But is anyone so low in intelligence that he cannot see this danger?

Second, it becomes more difficult, even if the above danger is not realized, to penetrate to thoughts of God if there is an intervening object of this nature. Man, being partly material, needs something beside a purely spiritual or mental image to help him think of God. Words must be employed to suggest the immaterial being of God. But the trouble with using images of the God being worshiped is that it becomes harder to escape from fixation on the image and get out into the pure realm of mental and spiritual imagination which is necessary if God, who is pure spirit, is to be adored.

If someone claims that we have the same problem with the word-symbol "G-O-D," we reply that there is a difference. The word does not purport to be a picture of God. We do not tend to associate finitude with God simply because the word representing His name is finite, because the word is not viewed as a picture or facsimile of Him. But the image does in some manner picture God, and we have to look at the image and say to ourselves, at the same time, that God is not limited as this picture of Him is—that He is not tangible as this idol. The question then becomes: What is the value of this image that it should be used in worship? The answer will be something like, "It helps men to think concretely of God." But we should not think concretely of God. He is not a concrete object; he is a universal spirit.

By way of defense, someone may ask: Is it not true that men, if they would worship God, must congregate in some one place and worship there? Call it a church, a synagogue, a temple, or whatever, is there not a necessary localization in divine worship? This is surely granted. However, this localization is not a localization of God, but merely of the place for worshiping God. If a man is going to worship, it is understood it must be in some place, but the Person whom he worships is not in any one place. And there should be nothing in his worship which would suggest that He is.

Does the fact that God prescribes the manner of His own worship mean that we dare do nothing at all in worship that is not specifically revealed by God? Does this mean that we may not worship at 11:00 on a Sunday morning without a special communication from heaven specifying that hour? Dare we settle what parts of worship are to precede or follow other parts unless God has dictated His directions about such matters? Dare we have an Easter sunrise service if there is no verse in the Bible which tells us so? Must we wait until an angel announces the proper hour before we can schedule a communion service?

The question seems perfectly legitimate. There can be no doubt that if God had revealed at what time we should worship, we would have no right to alter the hour. But inasmuch as there is no claimed revelation on this subject, we may assume that it has not been His pleasure to disclose any directives on the topic. What then are we to do? We know that God wants us to worship Him privately and publicly. We also shall see in the fourth commandment a specification of the day for public worship. But what about the hour? Nothing is said about that. What, then, shall we conclude? First, we should worship Him. Second, public worship should be on the Sabbath. Third, if there is to be worship it must be at some definite hour. Fourth, the hour not being specified, we must consult our own human interest, which dictates that it should be at the hour most convenient for most people. If that is 11:00, then the proper religious authorities must set that hour.

In other words, we may say that there are prescribed and unprescribed details of worship. Where they are prescribed, we dare not omit them or provide substitutions. Where they are not prescribed, we are obliged to develop these specifications in the general context of what is prescribed.

There is a mighty debate on the regulative principle. If it is not prescribed (by God), it is prescribed for worship (by men). We have mentioned one thing (time of worship service) that is not prescribed by God, and therefore must indubitably be determined by church officers. Some will say that dancing (illustrating a biblical doctrine or event) is not permitted because God has not specified it for His worship. On the other hand, others will say it is not the equivalent of preaching the Word if it visualizes words or events of Scripture? I'll let the reader work that out, only begging him to honor the conscientiousness of his opponent.

Chapter 6

The Third Commandment

"Thou shalt not take the name of the Lord thy God in vain; for the Lord will not hold him guiltless that taketh his name in vain" (Exodus 20:7).

The names of God in the Bible are more than mere designations. They not only denote, but connote as well. They indicate something of God's character or nature. The third prohibition, therefore, is not simply a prohibition against using one of the names of the deity profanely, but against irreverent reference to anything concerning the nature or decrees of God. A person may be profane without ever cursing, although he cannot curse without being profane. Simply disregarding the will of God in any matter is curseless profanity.

The word "vain" means empty, and so this commandment teaches that references to God must be meaningful and reverent. Thoughtless allusions to the deity or His ways are violations of this commandment. It is apparent that one may engage in such profanity while reciting the Apostles' Creed in church. What is commonly called profanity is only a more gross form of the same thoughtless reference to God and His ways. The excuse so commonly given—"he doesn't mean anything by it"—is not an excuse for profanity, but its very definition. Not meaning anything by the use of sacred language is exactly what constitutes the sin here forbidden.

How would men know apart from revelation that there is such a commandment as the third? That is, how could men know that they should not lightly think of or refer to the nature and being of God; that they should not use language loosely in such an important matter; that they should not profane the name of the Most Holy? Does the very asking of the questions not contain the answer? Do men not know that they should never use any language without meaning? Is it not obvious to all persons that communication is a device by which human society and many other human advantages are secured? If it is clear that speech and expression are useful abilities for men and society, is it not equally clear that the frustration of this ability is the opposite of a benefit, a type of curse, and the prostitution of a divine gift? If it is clear that men should not use any words in any context without meaning or purpose, is it not doubly clear that they should not take the name of their God in vain—that the name of the Most High is not to be used without thought or meaning?

If we know that speech is a way in which we may express our understanding of God and love for Him, then we know in the same thought that it is sinful not so to use our speech, and still more sinful to use it for the opposite purpose. Such reflections are so obvious that he who runs may read—and he does not have to read a book such as this one.

Is it excusable when a man using profanity does indeed mean something by it, but something other than what the words usually signify? We once heard a celebrated theologian justify the profane use of "hell" in a Christmas Eve scene in *A Tree Grows in Brooklyn.* According to a local custom, poor children who could not

afford Christmas trees would wait around on Christmas
Eve and often receive one free, when it was clear that it
was not going to be sold. One little urchin waited patiently, and the seller finally threw him a big tree that almost knocked the little fellow over. As the man threw the
tree he told the boy to get the hell out.

Under such circumstances, commented the theologian,
those words did not mean what they said at all, but
rather, they meant "God bless you." This comment calls
for comment. We admit readily that the benefactor did not
really mean what he said, but something vaguely in the
neighborhood of the charitable interpretation given it by
this theologian. But was it not profanity nonetheless?
Granted that the act was generous and that the man no
doubt meant well, was he not still guilty of a vain use of
God's "name"? Hell is the judgment of a righteous God,
and the word cannot be disrespected without God's judgments being disrespected. If no disrespect to God was intended, there was at least a vain use of language. Could
the tree have compensated for the bad example this man
set? Is it acceptable to be evil in speech as long as you
give good gifts?

Any complaints against providence would also constitute profaning God's name. To complain about the order
of things is to complain about the Orderer of them, is it
not? You may object that man and his sins pervert the
ways of God, and that a person may complain about this
perversion without complaining about the ordering of
God. True, we reply, if you complain *proximately* about
the disorders caused by man, but not if you complain *ultimately* about them.

Let me explain. Suppose you complain that this universe is, because of the evil of men, an evil universe,

badly contrived and regulated—that it should not have such disorder in it. In this case you are saying that the sovereign God, who has permitted a world to exist which includes sin, has made a mistake. Are you not reflecting either on his wisdom—that He has considered something good which is really evil, or right which is really wrong— or on His power, if He is unable to make things what He knows they ought to be rather than what they are? Is this not a profaning of His name, power, wisdom, goodness, or all these attributes of His being? Thus it is very possible for a person who has never "sworn" or "cussed," who has never been profane in the usual sense of that word, to be taking the name of the Lord his God in vain in a very refined and philosophical manner.

If we have seen above that it is possible for a person to be blessing when he seems to be cursing, we must note here that it is possible to be cursing when one seems to be blessing. That is, the person who finds fault with the universe, and thus with its Creator and Sustainer, is doing so in the presumed interests of goodness. In contrast, to fulfill this commandment, one must use the right words and the right thoughts in honoring God.

If a person does not believe this is the best possible world, he is intentionally or unintentionally profane. He may recognize the presence of sin, which does not belong in the ideal world. But if he believes in a sovereign God, he must also believe that this God brings His will to pass. If there is evil in the world the sovereign God has ordained, it must be in accord with an ultimate divine purpose. If God chose to permit rather than to prohibit it, there must have been some divine wisdom in that action. To think otherwise would seem to deny the omniscience, the goodness, or the power of God. All these thoughts would be forms of profanity.

A man may become indignant with his own sins and those of other persons, but at the same time he must view God's decision to permit these sins to exist as elements of God's wisdom. Indeed, if the man did not become indignant with sin, he would be profane. For God has created men free and responsible, and that opens up both the possibility and the responsibility of being indignant with sin. Not to be so, when the occasion calls for it, would be to disapprove of the constitution of nature. This illustration further indicates that profanity is a far-reaching concept, touching the secular as well as the sacred, and involving pious as well as blasphemous language.

The only way not to profane the name of God is to hallow it. Perhaps that is why the Lord's Prayer presents the positive form of this truth in its first petition: "Hallowed be Thy name." If we hallow God's name, we cannot profane it; conversely, if we do not hallow it, we necessarily profane it. We have a duty to hallow the name of God; not doing so is a failure of duty and, therefore, a profanation. Probably the commandment is given in the negative form because of our corruptions, not because any commandment can actually be fulfilled merely by avoiding something. Since we are prone to profanity, we are immediately warned against it: this behavior must be stopped. But then what? Its place must be filled with a wholesome, reverential spirit. If we may use an analogy, the fire must first be put out and then the ruins rebuilt. The house cannot be rebuilt while the fire is raging, and, on the other hand, putting out the fire leaves only a ruin, not a house.

In the Mosaic form of the ten commandments this third one has annexed to it the words, "for the Lord will not hold him guiltless that taketh his name in vain." We wonder why this particular commandment, and not the others, has this statement, "the Lord will not hold him guiltless," attached. Is it not true that God also will not hold those guiltless who have other gods in His presence? Similarly, He will not hold them guiltless who bow down and serve images. He will not hold them guiltless who violate the Sabbath, dishonor their parents, and so on. As we remarked in the chapter on sanctions, the moral law as a whole is enforced by nature and God; it is not only this one commandment the violation of which incurs punishment.

Could it be that the reason for the connection of the threat to this specific commandment is that it forbids a particularly gross form of immorality? Having any other god in the divine presence is the fundamental and root sin, to be sure. However, profaning God's name is perhaps the worst fruit of this root. A person who has another god alongside of God is capable of committing any sin when the two divinities come into conflict. But that capability is merely potential; it has not yet necessarily become actuality. It is certain to do so, but perhaps the first commandment is concerned with the initial sin rather than with its development. The development comes when the gods conflict, and the hating and profanation of the true God is how the spirit of the false worshiper is expressed.

There may be a second reason for associating this threat with the third commandment. Profanity is an ultimate expression of the repudiation of God. He is no longer merely neglected, disregarded, and subordinated, but He is actually abhorred and despised. To worship the creature rather than the Creator is, granted, a dreadful thing; but to despise the Creator is more dreadful still. If God is jealous about the purity of His worship, how must He feel about the wilful contamination and defiance of His commands?

A third reason, not necessarily related solely to the third commandment, is that God cannot mention too often that He is a consuming fire. Men are so prone to sentimental thinking, they are so disposed to bring their principles to agree with their lusts, they are so averse to suffering (even as they are inclined to do that which brings suffering), that they cannot be reminded too often that God is not mocked. He may appear to be asleep now (Psalm 44:23), the wicked may now flourish as the green bay tree (Psalm 37:35), and it may seem that God is indifferent to all the actions of men; but such is not the case, and this commandment reminds us of that fact. The deeds of men are recorded with a pen of iron (Jeremiah 17:1), and God will some day judge all men according to their works. He will not hold them guiltless of anything, though now it seems as if He holds them guiltless of everything. Since profanity is the ultimate mocking of God, the warning in this commandment constitutes a necessary reminder that however vain men's thoughts, words, and deeds may be, God's thoughts, words, and deeds will not be in vain.

Chapter 7

The Fourth Commandment

"Remember the sabbath day, to keep it holy. Six days shalt thou labor, and do all thy work; but the seventh day is the sabbath of the Lord thy God: in it thou shalt not do any work, thou, nor thy son, nor thy daughter, nor thy manservant, nor thy maidservant, nor thy cattle, nor thy stranger that is within thy gates: for in six days the Lord made heaven and earth, the sea, and all that in them is, and rested the seventh day: wherefore the Lord blessed the sabbath day, and hallowed it" (Exodus 20: 8–11).

This immediately raises the question: is there anything written in the nature of man which informs him that a seventh rather than a tenth or a third day should be thus hallowed? How is it plain to man, with or without revelation, that some day should be set aside for such a purpose? Well, is it not plain that there is a God, and that man owes allegiance to his Creator? You will grant that. Well then, should a man not show respect to this Creator? You will grant that too, but you will ask, "Why in such a visible manner?" The answer is that men are visible or physical creatures and express themselves in such ways. Proper sentiment of spirit might be sufficient for beings which are only spirits, but beings which have bodies as well, and which act and move and express themselves in these bodies, would be expected to show their spirit in an outward mode also.

"But why," you ask, "should a specific day be set aside?" Well, is it not apparent, even without special revelation, that all the time we have is a trust from our Creator and that we have it only because He allots it to us and only as long as He allots it to us? Is it not proper that some tangible recognition of this fact should be made?

"Very well," you acknowledge. "But if this is so, why not set aside all our days, since they all belong to God?" In one sense, indeed, we should do so. But since man is a finite and dependent creature who must work to meet his needs for existence, it is not reasonable to suppose that God would wish His creatures to commit suicide and extinguish the life He gives them by desisting from the labor without which they cannot survive. Accordingly, should not the giving of a regular portion of our days be the desideratum? And just as we would give a portion of our possessions and all other things, would we not give a portion of our time?

But we now come back to our original question. Would men know—could they know—apart from revelation that this regular portion, as far as time is concerned, is the setting aside of one day in seven? Presumably not, unless it was somehow known to man from the beginning of history that God had brought His world into being in six symbolic or actual days and then desisted from this work, and, furthermore, that He made that time of desisting to be a pattern guiding the creatures made in His image as to when they should desist from their work.

One form of the decalogue possibly supposes just such a tradition. If there was such a tradition, then it could be reasonably supposed that mankind, even without revelation, could know God's will in this matter and could therefore legitimately be expected to observe it. Otherwise we see no way by which men could be expected to know this. In that case, this would be the one part of the decalogue which could not be substantially known by natural law—and then only the exact period of time to be observed would be unknown, not that there should be some period of time.

Granted that some specified time should be set aside for God as an indication that all time belongs to Him, the question of how that time should be set aside now faces us. If we are already naturally obligated to redeem *all* time—to do whatever we do, whether we eat or drink, to the glory of God—how should be hallow the Sabbath especially?

In the first place, such hallowing would need to be more direct if it is to be special. That is, if in daily living we are obliged to do whatever we do as "unto the Lord," we would have the same obligation, but even more directly, on the Sabbath. On the other days we serve God by serving ourselves. We earn our daily bread and seek to honor Him in the way and the reason that we earn this bread. But still, it is *our* bread that we are earning; it is our own needs on which our activity immediately, if not ultimately, terminates. Should not Sabbath activity aim at God Himself, directly and immediately as well as ultimately? Should we not seek to worship God in His very presence and in His sanctuary, rather than through ourselves in our world of life and labor?

If the *method* of worshiping God on the Sabbath should be more direct than our worship of Him on other days, should not the *content* be more direct also? On the other six days we deal primarily with the data of natural revelation. That is, we are concerned with the secular

world, which of course is God's world and which reveals
much about God. If we are students, we are learning sci-
ence, literature, history, economics—all of which have
much to reveal about the ways of God. In studying various subjects we are studying God's natural revelation,
whether we have eyes to see it or not. But this is indirect
revelation; God is seen in the things He has made and
done, but not directly by His immediate communication.
If we are employed in the world of work we are watching
and participating in the outworking of God's providence,
and all this should be very instructive to us. But on the
Sabbath day we should attend to the direct revelation of
God, which He has been pleased to give us in the sacred
Scriptures. Here the Holy Spirit has given us His words
through inspired human agents, so that we know what
God is like, what His purposes in the world are, and how
we should interpret things while in this world. So this
day should be given to studying the Bible and anything
which would help to explain the meaning of the Bible,
that is, to wholesome religious literature and action.

Should a person read secular literature on the Lord's
Day? Is such reading consistent with keeping the
Sabbath holy? Granted that we can learn much about
God from such reading, is this different from the reading
of the week? Is it not still learning indirectly rather than
directly? Is this not immediately secular content (even
though the secular reveals much of the sacred) rather
than sacred?

There is a distinction between sacred and profane literature. As far as content is concerned, this is a difference
not of kind but of degree. But in the same way, the distinction between the worship of God on the Sabbath day
and His worship on other days is a difference not of kind

but of degree. The whole point of the Sabbath day, if it is to be special, is that it is different in this special degree. Presumably, this difference should apply to literature as well as to anything else, should it not?

Similarly, the other six days are devoted to the regular labor whereby we earn our subsistence. (Students are in effect "earning their subsistence" too, inasmuch as school is something of an apprenticeship for life and, therefore, a part of learning one's way in the world.) But if we do regular labor on the Lord's Day, is the Lord's Day still special? Is it not rather our own day?

Someone may question our logic with a question concerning religious literature. He may ask: "Granted that religious literature which helps us to understand the revelation of God is a legitimate activity for the Sabbath day, what about the book I am holding in my hand? It is a religious book. It purports to explain some aspects of the biblical revelation and to help persons understand the nature of God and their duty to Him. Is this legitimate reading for the Sabbath day?" We would think so. But then he says, "This is our text for a course in ethics. It is therefore part of our weekday duty. It belongs to the six days. Can it legitimately belong to the seventh?"

Let me respond with my own question. Does the fact that this book, and others like it, are used on the other six days of the week for study purposes change the character of the book somehow? Apparently not. It still remains a book on religion even though it is used in courses during the week. Its character is not thereby changed. So we see no reason why it could not be studied on the Sabbath, as a book on mathematics could not be.

The situation here is something like that of a minister who works on Sunday—perhaps harder than on any other day, as that is the day of his special duties. Yet it is apparent that there is no violation of the Sabbath law in that work, inasmuch as he is a necessary instrument of human worship. The very Sabbath command could not be kept unless the minister worked on the Sabbath. The very law which forbids others engaged in unnecessary labor to work on that day obliges him to work. So, in the same way, a religion book, while of course it does not need to be read only on the Sabbath, could be read on that day because it is consistent with the purpose of that day.

We have asked about studying on the seventh day; what about other work? Well, again we notice that all legitimate work is a way of knowing and serving God. But still there is a distinction between working for God directly and indirectly. Since the Sabbath is a special day, distinguished from the other six, ordinary indirect service is not required or permitted on the Sabbath, but only direct service of God—unless, in the nature of things, the secular work in question simply must be done all the time, including Sundays.

Let us consider what types of work exist which must be done on Sunday as well as on other days. For example, you are probably reading this book by artificial light. Our entire economy is based on the use of artificial light. We could not get along normally without it. But to keep such lights going on Sundays involves some persons in work. Much of the lighting industry may and should be closed down on Sundays, but it is evident that the whole industry could not be closed. Some persons must work in such an industry, not in the interests of making more money, but due to the necessities of our culture. Similarly, a great modern steel mill could not close down completely on Sunday without setting the plant's work back for days. A skeleton force of men is needed for Sunday work. Many other instances of this sort are obvious.

But much work that is said to be necessary, the claim to be such is questionable. For example, we just referred to the undisputed necessity that a skeleton crew remain on duty at the steel mill. Does this justify the entire mill working on Sunday? Certainly not.

Let me mention a specific incident from my own experience. Between college and seminary I worked in a large steel mill that employed thousands of men. My job was in the pay office, five and a half days a week. Near the end of the month I was informed that I would have to work on a Sunday in order to get the paychecks out and balance the books.

I asked my immediate superior why it was necessary to work on Sunday. Would not one or two Saturday afternoons accomplish the same thing? He said he could not answer the question. I replied that I had to have an answer before I would know whether I could work on Sunday. He referred me to his superior, saying my question was not typically raised.

The head of the department then called me in and asked me to state my question, which I did once again. He replied that he supposed it was not really necessary to work on Sundays; the tasks could be done some other time. But that was the way things were done.

I explained that I could not agree to work on Sunday if the work was not strictly necessary and justifiable. He said that in that case I would not work at all. So I walked out of the room without a job. Later the company relented and permitted me to retain my job without working on Sundays, on the grounds that I was a preministerial student. I did not accept the reasoning for their ruling, but I retained the job.

Someone will object, "That was all right for you to have run the risk of losing your job. After all, you had no family to support." True, but I did have myself to support, and no family was supporting me. But still, I grant the point that my situation was not nearly so tense as it would have been had I carried a responsibility for defendants.

But what are we to draw from this? Is it wrong to violate the Sabbath regulation if you are single, but okay if you are married? Or wrong if you are merely married, but permissible if you have children? What is the determining factor in this situation? Are we to do only necessary work on the Sabbath day, except whenever there is an economic necessity to do unnecessary work? Does the end justify the means—does self-preservation justify violating the law of God? Or if not self-preservation, is the preservation of others sufficient reason?

If this is so with respect to the fourth commandment, the same guideline would presumably apply to all other commandments also, and to the whole moral law. Does this mean then that the end justifies the means, and that the rightness or wrongness of any action is determined not by God but by man? Does the survival of man, rather than the commands of God, become our governing principle? In other words, does the moral law of God hold only up to the point where its observance challenges our existence?

Let us test this principle. First, it clearly would make man, not God, ultimate. It would tie God's hands. He could command us, but only up to a point. The creature would be telling God how far He could go.

Second, if man's life becomes more ultimate than God's command, then are we not worshiping the creature rather than the Creator? After all, the one to whom we give our ultimate allegiance is the object of our worship. So this principle would be just as much a form of idolatry as any practice which employed images.

Third, if man's preservation were ultimate, why would his mere welfare not also be? If his life is so sacred that it cannot morally be violated even by God Himself, why then would it not be his idol throughout? If so, it would follow that he need never do anything that God commands unless he supposes that it is good for him and sees to his own satisfaction that it is. If this is an inevitable implication of the position stated, then this principle completely subverts the moral foundations and totally displaces God.

Fourth, if this principle were true, how could God ever test anyone morally? As already indicated, there could be no meaning in the acid test of life. Where would there be any meaning? How could a nonultimate God justify the testing of an ultimate man? Indeed Man should become the tester of god, not God the tester of man.

So far all that we have found to be appropriate activity on the Sabbath day is the reading of the Word of God and expositions thereof. But there is more to the service of God than reading about Him. There is the actual worship of His name. We will discuss church membership and worship more particularly in chapter 16.

Also, there is more to the service of God than learning of Him and worshiping Him. There is also expressing His gracious nature. The Germans call good deeds *Liebestätigkeiten*, love deeds. They are deeds which flow from love, essentially the love of God. Of course, these should be done on other days than the Sabbath—and so should worship, for that matter. But both worship and service are preeminently in order on the Sabbath day. These are so important that they have a place on this hallowed day. Work cannot be justified unless it is absolutely necessary, but doing deeds of kindness is so indispensably a part of true worship that it belongs on the day of the Lord. Hence the soundness of the tradition that works of worship, absolute necessity, and mercy are proper (and only they) on the sabbath day.

Chapter 8

The Fifth Commandment

"Honor thy father and they mother: that thy days may be long upon the land which the Lord thy God giveth thee" (Exodus 20:12).

A child begins his life as a dependent creature, probably the most dependent of all creatures in their infancy. He is the least fit to survive of all animals. His very first duty, if he is to survive, is obedience. He must obey or perish. For example, if he does not do as others direct he will drink poison, throw himself down the stairs, drown in the tub, or roast on the fire. He is incapable of understanding anything, least of all his danger. His is not to reason why; his is but to do or die.

Furthermore, if he would survive, the tot must learn *instant* obedience. If a child who lives in the country is about to step on a sleeping snake and his father tells him to stand motionless and not take one step further but to freeze immediately where he is, he must obey or die. If he decides to take just a couple more steps and then stop, it may be too late.

Moreover, he must learn *exact* obedience. We know of a child in India who was climbing down a mountainside and became trapped on a ledge. His parents heard his cry and, running to the edge of the mountain, immediately saw their child's predicament. They told their child, who was only five years old, to remain exactly where he was and not move at all, for any motion could cause a fatal fall. This child had been trained in exact obedience, and that is why he was still there when a man was lowered down to him on a rope and rescued him.

When does a person become free from the need to obey? The answer, I think, is never. To reach this conclusion, let us continue to trace the evolution of each individual human. As a child grows up he learns why he should not touch the stove, lean over the banister, and the like. His own sense of self-preservation may then take over, insofar as prohibitions of this kind are concerned. He no longer needs to be told not to drink poison or swallow safety pins. Is he now free from the laws of obedience? Hardly. He is only free from their articulation in certain forms. He is under obligation not to eat poison and swallow pins just as much as ever, and even more. He still has the prohibition from his parents, and in addition he now has the prohibition from his own intelligence as well. After a while he will also learn about the civil laws that prohibit suicide. In time he will perhaps learn that God, his Creator, is on the side of these prohibitions too. Instead of becoming free from the necessity of obedience, each passing year he becomes more bound to it.

Obedience pervades the cycle of human life. For example, as you read about obedience at this moment you are probably reading in obedience to some command: your professor's (if you are a student), or your father's (if he is a friend of the author), or the necessity of giving a speech or presenting a paper, or curiosity in the realm of ethics which commands you to read anything in the field that may be useful to you. (It is a consoling thought to a writer on ethics that if anyone reads his book at all, that person will do so for some ethical reason, whether he is aware of that reason or not.)

If we agree that there must be authority and obedience in any situation, who shall be the authority and who shall obey? In the case of the infant there can be no doubt of the answer. His parents bring him into the world; by the laws of man, nature, and God, they have him in their care. They must provide for him and prepare him to face the world on his own at some later date. Can there be any doubt that they have the right and duty to regulate the child's life, and that this involves authority on their part and obedience on his?

Perhaps a few thinkers may challenge this proposition. Some feel, in the spirit of Romanticism, that the child has some inner drives of his own which are sacred and should be permitted free expression. They would argue that these impulses should not be restrained or directed by others, not even by parents. But very few will hold this principle without qualification. If, for example, a toddler happens upon a gun and feels an inner urge to pull the trigger while aiming at himself—or perhaps at the person who thinks the child should be totally uninhibited—this will be probably be passed off as one of those "exceptions that prove the rule." This and similar examples are indeed exceptions and they do prove the rule, but the rule they prove is that the parents—and, in emergencies, any adult—must direct the child's activities.

What about obedience after the child begins to grow up and no longer thinks or behaves as a child? Is he still under his parents' authority? Of course he is. Parents do not, when the child reaches age ten or twelve, suddenly permit him to drink poison. He is still forbidden. The difference now, as we noted above, is that he no longer

needs to be told not to drink poison, both because he
knows they feel that way and because he feels that way
himself. However, let him ever become morbidly suicidal
in mood and attempt to do away with himself by this
method, and his parents, if they manage to prevent it, will
likely deal quite severely with him.

Even as some duties becomes tacitly assumed, others
remain explicit. Suppose the child, now a teenager, wants
to go to an all-night party. Who decides whether he can
go? Shall we say that the teenager should make his own
decision, since he is old enough to know what is involved? Most teenagers, and many parents, think so. If
the parent and the teenager are in agreement about
whether he should go to the party, there is no problem of
authority. Or, if they differ, perhaps the difference can be
resolved cooperatively; perhaps the parents can convince
the teenager that their view is right, or the teenager, by
presentation of additional factors, can bring the parents
to his side.

But suppose there remains an impasse. Then what?
There are only two possibilities here: either the teenager's
will prevails or the parents'. Which should it be? There
are arguments on each side. The teenager may argue that
it is his own life, and that he should have the right to run
it as he sees fit, even if he makes mistakes. He might say
that his parents should not be the only ones allowed to
make mistakes; he should have the privilege too. This is
probably the teenager's ultimate argument, though he
may also contend that all his friends are doing this sort of
thing, the party will be chaperoned, the school authorities are permitting it, he will be considered all varieties of
oaf if he is not permitted to go, and various other appeals

which young people are known to make with considerable cogency and passion.

What is the case for the parents' authority? They obviously cannot dispute that it is the teenager's life, not their own. They may also grant that the behavior in question is generally accepted by the teenager's peers, whose opinion of him (they must also admit) means a great deal to him. They may say they sympathize with their son, or even wish they could be persuaded by his argument, which they have considered objectively and not with closed or prejudiced minds. But they have not been convinced, and therefore they cannot grant permission and their son must obey their unwelcome prohibition.

Why? Because, although the parents have made, and will presumably continue to make, mistakes in every area of life (including the administration of their family), they are, in the nature of the case, less likely to make mistakes than their teenage children. There is such a thing as wisdom that comes with age and can come in no other way. The parents were not necessarily any wiser as children than their own children are, but they are necessarily wiser now. Someone's will must prevail in the family, unless anarchy and chaos are desirable, and since the parents' will is the one more likely to be wise, their will must prevail.

The parents will insist upon prevailing not because they desire their own will, but because they desire the good. They desire not to frustrate their child's will, but to frustrate the folly that would probably result from its free expression. They will recite those hallowed words of parents: "This hurts me more than it hurts you, but it will do both of us good."

As an additional note, let us also point out that it is not appropriate to hold a "family conference" to decide the issue. This would presuppose that even though children are not as wise as their parents, adding their inexperience to the equation will be helpful in reaching a decision. We are not saying that family discussions to help parents understand situations and make better decisions are wrong, but in these discussions the parents' authority must not be challenged or replaced. Otherwise, in the family conference, it will be the total family, including the children and not only the parents, who share the authority.

Thus far we have mentioned the "parents' will," as if it is uniform. But suppose the two parents differ. What then? We are asking not what actually happens in such a case, but what *should* happen. We have established that the boy's will should not prevail over his parents, but which parent's will should prevail over the other?

Let us first note that one of the parent's wills must prevail. Decisions must be made, and in some cases, such as whether a child goes to a party or not, there is no intermediate position. We cannot say "Let the wiser parent decide," for it is obvious that the two authorities are divided on who is wiser. No one will favor bringing in some external authority to settle such disputes, for it is inconceivable that an authority would be available to troubleshoot all the differences of opinion that arise between fathers and mothers.

No, father or mother must prevail. Who should it be? We say father's will must prevail, for several reasons. First, mothers usually prefer it that way, at least those who realize that democracy does not work under all domestic circumstances. We have conducted no Gallup poll on this subject, but we have discussed this issue in many places, and we find women generally in favor of the men being the head of the home and complaining that men are unwilling to assume that responsibility.

Second, tradition favors this option. The henpecked husband is a sorry figure. Even—perhaps especially—women find him pitiable. While public opinion does not tolerate brutality or wifebeating, there remains a general feeling that it is right for the man to assume the lead.

Third, although far more mothers have entered the world of business and industry than ever before, many still remain at home. Even professional women, with few exceptions, spend more time at home than their husbands, who are more involved in the affairs of the world. This gives one a lesser and the other a greater opportunity to be conversant with things in general and more able to make decisions.

Fourth, women are normally much more involved emotionally than men. Men, probably as a result of their psychology, are more detached and unperturbed and better able to make judgments.

Fifth, the physical strength of men is not irrelevant here. To be sure, might does not make right, but it is essential to enforcing the right. We are not hinting that men should lead because they could force their will anyway. What we mean is that since law always involves sanctions, as we have already shown in a general way, and since men more than women is able by natural constitution to apply these sanctions, this seems to be a hint from the Creator that man is to make the decisions.

Sixth, if the revelation of the Bible is true, there can be no argument on the matter and there is no need for other reasons. The Bible is explicit on this point.

Let us hasten to point out, before leaving this brief discussion, that the husband's headship in the family does not include any right to tyrannize over his family. Nor does it mean that he should not consult wife or children. It does not even imply that the other family members, especially his wife, may not in many instances have superior wisdom which he should consult and adopt as his own policy.

We have restricted ourselves here to the family relationship. It is the center of all human operations and is the place where the authority principle first finds expression. Therefore, it is specifically cited in this fifth commandment. However, what begins in the home by no means ends there. On the contrary, the authority principle applies throughout all the relationships of life. Everyone is the superior authority at some points and inferior at others. We all must learn both how to rule and how to obey. This is the stuff that holds family, nation, and world together. Therefore this commandment is the first one with a promise: "That thy days may be long upon the land which the Lord thy God giveth thee" (Exodus 20:12).

Chapter 9

The Sixth Commandment

"Thou shalt not kill" (Exodus 20:13).

We have indicated (in chapter 2) why murder, in the nature of things, is to be abhorred and why any disposition which tends toward it is also to be abhorred. Let us here face the question of what our attitude toward the murderer should be.

It is apparent that we cannot detect with certainty the inwardly angry and hateful person. We do not know what goes on in the hearts of men. We may surmise from some actions and words, but we cannot gain direct or certain knowledge about such matters. We can disapprove of such attitudes, but we can hardly do more than that. Or, even if we were able to detect the slightest presence of this root of murder, we could hardly do anything about it unless we did something about the entire human race. For who is totally free of all unjust anger, tendencies to slight others, and even hatred on occasion? So, either because we cannot know specifically or because we know too much generally, we cannot do anything about this hidden sin except exhort and pray about it.

What shall we do when this disposition expresses itself in an overt action of killing? First, we must be sure that the perpetrator of the given act is indeed a responsible and guilty person. Imagine a mentally deranged maniac who breaks loose with an axe. Blood flows, men die. Horrible, tragic, ghastly! You instinctively express aesthetic and emotional horror at the deed; but are you morally enraged? Would any judge or jury find such an obviously deranged person guilty of first-degree murder?

Think of a soldier in battle. He kills as effectively as any gangster. His victims are just as dead. Is his killing a vice to be hated? On the contrary, it is generally regarded as a virtue to be praised, even though the same deed when committed by a gangster is a crime.

Or suppose a medical doctor accidentally administers a wrong dosage. The patient dies. This is terrible indeed, and the patient is just as dead as if an enemy had slain him in cold blood, deliberately and cruelly. But can anyone consider this innocent killing an evil deed?

The point should be clear: the act of killing is itself neither good, bad, nor indifferent. It takes on moral significance only in relation to its source. If that source is nonmoral (e.g., a hurricane), the killing is nonmoral. If the source is moral but irresponsible (e.g., a maniac), the killing is nonmoral. If the source is moral, responsible, and in the path of duty (e.g., a soldier or a public executioner), the killing is a virtue. If the source is moral, responsible, and outside the path of duty (e.g., a gangster), then, and only then, does killing become morally evil.

So, then, we must first assure ourselves by fair trial that a morally responsible person is guilty of deliberate killing. If such is the case, then what is society supposed to do? It seems to us as clear as that the sun rose this morning that the killer should be killed.

We need not rehearse here the evidence for sanctions and their necessity. We consider it evident, in the law of nature and in the law of revelation, that wrongdoing must be punished. This is part of the common consciousness and conscience of mankind. We admit that there are many, especially in our day, who do not grant that this doctrine is true or universal. When their position is examined, however, it is seen that they are not really challenging this doctrine as much as challenging the fact of murder. By this we mean, not that they deny that some persons kill others, but that they deny that some persons kill others inexcusably.

If the situation were indeed as these objectors see it, we and all men would agree with their opposition to capital punishment. If there were no murders—that is, no inexcusable killings—we would agree that no one should suffer capital punishment. We all agree that a man should not be punished for something he did not do; therefore, we agree that a person who did not inexcusably kill another person should not be executed on the assumption that he did. As is often the case, the moral principles at play in this debate are the same on both sides, but the moral judgments differ because the intellectual judgments differ. The area of disagreement is not morality, properly speaking, but empirical fact.

Opponents of capital punishment give various reasons for exonerating killers and denying that they are murderers in the proper sense of that term. For instance, many opponents argue that men are the products of their environment and are unable to act any differently than their background dictates. Thus, "dead-end kids" reared in the conventions of the jungle have no scruples about killing. Murder to them is not wrongdoing; it is merely an application of the natural law of self-preservation. In other words, according to this line of thinking, some murderers at least are really no different from animals. They know no more than animals, and we should be no more indignant at their killing a schoolmate than we would be at a lion for devouring an antelope.

Others think that some persons' heredity drives them, by various compulsions to kill. They are not really free agents at all, but do what glands or internal forces beyond their wilful control impel them to do.

In one form or another, the opponents of capital punishment seek to remove blame from the supposed culprit. They may even argue, if following the defense that men are the products of their environment, claim that the judges who hear the case and all the members of society who appoint them to do so are as guilty as the culprit. After all, had they been in the killer's circumstances, they would have done as he did, and if he were in their circumstances he would not have done as he did.

To summarize, the basic argument by opponents of capital punishment is that the murderer is not really guilty as charged, or if he is, so are his judges, and therefore if he is punished they should be punished also. Since this is not feasible, the murderer should not be punished because they are not. As a bonus, the additional argument may be presented that punishment would not do any good anyway.

These are admittedly cogent considerations, and they require adequate refutation. With respect to the claim that killers, because of their background in inheritance and environment, are unable to do other than what they did, we can do no better than to cite the words of Jonathan Edwards: "A man can't be truly said to be unable to do a thing, when he can do it if he will." That is, if a man does not resist killing simply because he does not will to restrain himself, this does not justify our saying that he is unable to resist killing. This would be an abuse of the word "inability." No matter what his background or heredity may be, if it remains within his natural power to choose not to murder, he must be held guilty if he does. His heredity may be whatever it is, and his environment as barbaric as can be imagined, but if they leave his will intact, he is a responsible person.

Can anyone deny that a person is responsible for his acts so long as he is able to do as he wills or chooses? That is, if a person was capable of willing not to kill another person and restraining his hand, would he not be guilty if he did not restrain his hand? If a man raises his hand against his brother because he wills to do so, can there be any doubt that he is responsible for what he did? Only if his heredity or environment removed from him the power to do as he willed could he be exonerated from blame.

Indeed, this is what heredity or environment does in the case of the insane person: they make it impossible for the person to do as he may will to do, or they may even take from him the use of his will altogether. In such a case, the person is clearly not responsible for any crime he may have committed. Society, while it may be compelled to confine him, would have no grounds to punish him. But unless this is the case—unless the person has lost the power of will altogether or has lost the ability to do what he does will—does he not remain responsible? If not, what is the meaning of responsibility anyhow? And in whom *does* it remain?

As we noted above, there is one more objection. Even if our opponents were persuaded by these considerations, they would likely ask, "In any case, supposing that these persons are guilty as charged, what good is capital punishment going to do them? Are their wills going to be strengthened thereby? How does society free itself of the onus of having cast the stone at someone for a sin of which all persons are at least inwardly guilty themselves?"

In answer to these questions, let us submit several observations. First, if it is evident that a guilty man ought to suffer for his crimes, as we believe we have adequately shown, is it not also clear that he should suffer proportionately to them? If crime should be punished at all, it should be punished according to its measure: small crime, small punishment; large crime, large punishment. The truth of this claim seems as obvious as the obverse is—namely, that it is wrong to punish a man heavily for a small crime or lightly for a large one. If a starving person is sentenced to ten years for stealing a loaf of bread while another man kills his doting mother and receives a slap on the wrist, is this not outrageous? It is outrageous not because these are not punishments for crimes—for indeed they are—but because they are out of all proportion to the crimes. Applying the principle of "an eye for an eye and a tooth for a tooth" (which Christ did not condemn, as we will show shortly) to murder, what conclusion can be drawn than that there should be a life for a life?

Confinement to an institution is not the equivalent of forfeiting one's life. Some will say that it is actually worse, and that some murderers would prefer execution over life imprisonment; but, if so, then the sentence of confinement is unfair in being too severe. An eye for an eye, a life for a life. If confinement is less or more severe than murder—and it is surely one or the other, as no one claims it is an exact equivalent—then it does not fit the crime in punishment of which it is administered.

Second, the doctrine of capital punishment has been a part of the common conviction of mankind. The rule of death for murder is found in virtually all law codes. And, as we have shown, it is not really challenged even by those who seem to oppose it, for they oppose not the punishment itself but the definition of the crime. They insist that the person is not really guilty as charged, but they do not deny that if he were, in the ultimate sense, he should be punished proportionately.

Third, the supernatural revelation of God teaches this. Some claim otherwise, actually citing this sixth commandment, "Thou shalt not kill," against capital punishment. Such an interpretation would remove the only proportionate punishment for killing, namely, a life for a life. The commandment is directed to the entire Hebrew community, stating that no one should take another's life. If someone should violate this command, what is to be done? This commandment does not answer that question. The associated Mosaic legislation does answer it, however. "A life for a life" is its precept, and numerous laws within the Mosaic code indicate when a person was to be killed by divine commandment.

In its context, therefore, it is evident that the sixth commandment forbids people to take the life of *innocent* people, and that the consequences of disobedience are spelled out in the fuller codification of the law. That consequence, in many cases, was capital punishment. If God is not contradicting Himself on alternate pages of the Old Testament, He assumes we will understand that the sixth commandment forbids unjustifiable murder and that the sanctions delivered in the Mosaic law authorized the magistrates to execute justifiable capital punishment.

Christ did indeed repudiate "an eye for an eye" and told his followers to turn the other cheek. That His remarks, too, are to be taken in their context, just as the sixth commandment must be read in context, is obvious. If we take this teaching in the context of Christ's life and behavior, what do we find? We find that He did not overthrow the civil courts, as Tolstoy thought He should have done. He did not require soldiers to give up their uniforms when they were converted, as He would have had to do had He thought killing under all circumstances was wrong. He would not have advised His disciples to render unto Caesar that which was Caesar's if the fighting of wars, suppressing of revolts, and executing of criminals were morally evil. Nor could He have rebuked those who smote Him had He meant the teaching of "turn the other cheek" to have no qualifications whatsoever.

What, then, did Christ mean? Since it is apparent that He did not mean to do away with law, order, punishment, and war, we may find the explanation in relation to the common view of the law of retaliation in His time. Men taught and thought that, since this principle of eye for eye was the ideal canon of justice and the guide for human judges, it should be applied privately as well as in public matters. Thus they felt justified in bearing grudges and in getting even, feeling that virtue required retaliation against ever slight they ever suffered from anyone, under any circumstances at any time, and that forgiveness was a violation rather than an expression of virtue. Christ declared otherwise. In principle, He taught, while this law of eye for eye is ideal for the courts and must be maintained by the powers that be, and should be respected by His disciples, it does not follow that it can never be waived. On the contrary, He required His disciples to waive it whenever possible and, instead of seeking vengeance, to give way to the offender, to bear injustice, to return good for evil, to turn the other cheek. This sublime teaching at once does justice to the ideal of an eye for an eye and the principle of mercy as well, each in its proper place.

For a discussion of the application of the sixth commandment to war, we refer the reader to chapter 22.

Chapter 10

The Seventh Commandment

"Thou shalt not commit adultery" (Exodus 20:14).

Christ's exposition of this commandment will be the foundation of our discussion. He said, "Ye have heard that it was said by them of old time, Thou shalt not commit adultery; but I say unto you, that whosoever looketh on a woman to lust after her hath committed adultery with her already in his heart" (Matthew 5:27–28).

When Christ said, "It was said by them of old time, Thou shalt not commit adultery; but I say unto you . . . ," He was not, of course, taking issue with the law of God given at Sinai. He had previously said that He came not to destroy the law but to fulfill it. Furthermore, it would be very strange if the servant of God should criticize the law of God. Indeed, Christ was the agent of revelation in the Old Testament, and the vision Moses had of God was nothing less than a vision of the preincarnate manifestation of Christ. Only the second person of the Godhead has ever become visible: "No man hath seen God at any time; the only begotten Son, which is in the bosom of the Father, He hath declared Him" (John 1:18).

It would be very strange if Christ in the New Testament contradicted what He had revealed in the Old Testament. No, when He says with implied disapproval, "It was said by them of old time, Thou shalt not commit adultery," He means to indict the interpretation that the

rabbis of old, not Moses, gave to this seventh commandment. This is quite analogous to His comment on the
sixth commandment: "It was said by them of old time,
Thou shalt not kill; . . . but I say unto you" (Matthew
5:21–22). Again He is not taking issue with Moses, but
with Moses's commentators. He is not disagreeing with
the sixth or seventh commandment, but with the
prevailing interpretations that had robbed these
commandments of much of their power.

The rabbinic interpretations of both these commands
were wrong in being superficial. They were right as far as
they went, but they did not go far enough. They did not,
as a matter of fact, go a step further than natural man was
morally able to go; not a step further than a man could go
without a new heart; not a bit further than any sinner
could go in external conformity. They stopped at the first
level of meaning—the act itself. "Thou shalt not kill"
meant purely "Thou shalt not take another man's life by
murder." They saw no further than that. The man who
stopped short of literal murder was no violator of the
sixth commandment. Similarly, the person who did not
commit the literal act of adultery was no violator of the
seventh commandment.

In contrast, Christ taught that a violation of the
commandment begins in the heart. Just as murder originates in anger without cause, so adultery begins with
looking at a woman to lust after her. Neither anger nor
lust need ever express itself in an overt act at all; yet, in
each instance, the man has violated the commandment.

This interpretation by Christ digs even deeper than
the area of thought or intention. A plan to commit murder or adultery is clearly a violation of the commandment,
though it may be visible only to God and to the person

sinning. Prior to that, a man may feel unjustified anger without taking thought of how he will express that anger, or he may feel lust without ever proceeding to a plan of gratification. But before even that stage is reached, there must be a disposition to evil—an angry or an adulterous heart. Christ condemns original sin itself, or the place where sin originates. He is putting His axe at the root of moral evil: the evil heart.

Christ's definition of adultery, then, is this: any illegitimate sexual relation or the desire for it. The action itself is, of course, condemned; but far more than that is condemned. The very desire for the illegitimate act is sin. Lust is the baby, and illicit intercourse is the grown man, but both are stages in the life cycle of the same sin—adultery—and the person guilty of either is an adulterer.

It is interesting that Christ works toward the less obvious rather than the more obvious types of violation. That is, He does not find it necessary to say that homosexuality or other forms of perversion violate this commandment. It should be obvious to all that if some forms of heterosexuality, which are in line with the nature of man, are adulterous, certainly any form of homosexuality, which is contrary to the very nature of man, is also adultery. After all, adultery, as the word is commonly used, is only a violation of positive law, not of natural law. It is natural for man and woman to cohabit, but God has set down certain positive regulations to control with whom one may cohabit: it is to be between the same man and the same woman, within wedlock. Homosexuality, on the other hand, is totally out of the natural pattern. Sexual gratification in any other way than heterosexually is unnatural.

God often assumes unnatural acts to be sinful rather than legislating explicitly against them. In Romans 1:26–27, Paul cites as evidence of the utmost degradation that men turn from the natural use of woman and lust one toward another, men with men doing that which is unseemly. The Bible says very little about this common perversion of both ancient and modern paganism, because it is so obviously evil. God is represented as the God of nature, the Creator of natural laws. These natural laws are to be respected as expressions of God's will. Men do not need any special legislation in order to know the unnatural to be evil.

Again, as we began to say before that digression, Christ, in His commentary on the moral law, does not go from the obvious to the more obvious, from the known to the better known. Rather, He moves toward what is less obvious. He starts with points that men acknowledge and then shows them what is implied in this acknowledgment. Murder they all recognize, so He will not bother to point out how it is even more unnatural to murder one's parents. Instead He points out that unjustified anger is made of the same stuff as murder. Christ does not point out what even the corrupted nature of man cannot altogether forget; He insists on what the corrupted nature of man is too coarse to think of unless obliged to do so. Likewise, if adultery is wrong, Christ does not speak of sexual perversion which even the heathen know is wrong, but of lust which even the so-called righteous are prone to overlook.

While the seventh commandment requires purity of heart and forbids sex only when it falls outside the area of divine permission (i.e., marriage), this area of marriage is closely hemmed in. Christ permitted no divorce "saving for the cause of fornication" (Matthew 5:32). He did not require divorce even for that sin, but clearly permitted it should the innocent party demand it. Here, by "fornication" our Lord no doubt refers to the outward act, and not merely to lust from which that act proceeds, and which is also of the nature of fornication. So imperative is the maintenance of sexual purity that infidelity can actually dissolve the otherwise indissoluble marriage.

Christ does not Himself give further moral direction to regulate physical relationships within marriage, but left it to His apostle, Paul, to complete the biblical instruction. Paul adds in 1 Corinthians two further teachings which round out the Christian conception of sex. Even within the framework of marriage, one is not completely free to do whatever one wishes. Christians are advised to withhold themselves by mutual restraint in order to keep their bodies under control and not become the slaves of a fundamentally legitimate relationship. The second Pauline instruction is related to this first one: while couples may abstain from intercourse only by mutual consent, on the other hand, so basic is the sexual relationship that neither party is to defraud the other, but to consider himself as belonging to the other.

But if all men, including even converted men, who have true love for God in their hearts, maintain the remnants of an evil, corrupt nature, then all men must be guilty of violating this exceedingly strict command of Christ (and, indeed, all the exceedingly strict commands of God). If this is so, then why does Christ command them? This question is pertinent to all the commandments, but we will consider it with reference to the strict seventh commandment.

With respect to the unconverted, the law is meant to bring us to Christ. Christ as Lawgiver intends to bring us to Christ as Savior. Men are prone to trust in their own righteousness and will continue to do so until they are exposed for what they are. They have an excuse for all their sins, and they exonerate themselves of every violation of the law, so that in the end they are not sinners at all. No natural man ever truly believes himself to be guilty before a holy God. Certainly, no natural man who has a veneer of religion thinks so.

Naturally, a person who thinks he has kept the law is not going to be interested in someone who offers himself as a savior from sin. Rather, he will resent such a person. He not only feels he has no need for such a savior, but he must regard this person as a menace to morals. For him, salvation comes by keeping the law, and not by believing or trusting in some savior. Nothing will change this person's mind, except a revelation of what the law really teaches. Saul of Tarsus was not converted until the "law came and sin revived and I died" (see Romans 7:9); that is, the real meaning of the law came home to him. The sin was there all the time, but was silenced by his imagined conformity to the law. When it revived, he, instead of being self-assured and confident, felt dead in humiliation and guilt. Paul thus came out from a misunderstanding of the law of Moses which was then current among his teachers and into an understanding of the law of Moses as given by Christ on the mount in Galilee. When he thus understood the law, he came to the Savior and he preached the same to others.

Now Christ is saying to every unconverted person, "Here is what holiness really is." If you hope by your performance to stand before God, then understand what

God requires. *Everything* must be good: your very nature, all your imaginations and thoughts, every action with respect to duties to be done and sins to be avoided—all the time, in every place, under every circumstance. He who offends in one point offends in all. Every idle word shall be brought into the judgment. If you want salvation by keeping of the law—here is the law; walk ye in it. Such a law slays the unconverted immediately, so that Christ may make him alive.

But what is the function of the law of Christ in the hearts of true believers? In the first place, it continues to convict them of their own depravity of nature. Although they are converted, they are not yet completely sanctified. Though they now love Christ, they still also hate Him. Though they now trust in Him, they still have traces of self-trust left. Though they now love virtue, they still have principles of vice within them. The law is constantly searching them, exposing them, humbling them. It is meant to do that. The Christian life is a life of penitence. True Christians are those who mourn.

The sweet irony is that the unconverted, who have nothing but sin in their hearts, are utterly unconscious of it, while the converted, who have the seed of their new and holy life, are constantly chastened because of their remaining sin. The sinner who needs Christ most of all never comes to Him, while the saint comes to Him all the time. The sinner who has no righteousness glories in what he thinks he has, while the saint glories only in the Lord his righteousness. A Christian who boasts in his own goodness is a contradiction in terms. Either he is no Christian, or he cannot boast in his own righteousness. "By grace are ye saved . . . not of works, lest any man should boast" (Ephesians 2:8–9).

The second purpose of the law in the life of the saint is to show him his duty to Christ. "If ye love me, keep my commandments" (John 14:15). Here are His commandments. If any man really would come after Christ, let him deny himself, take up his cross, and follow. Christ is his Savior; but Christ the Savior is also Christ the Lawgiver. There are not two Christs, but only one. If we trust in Christ the Savior we will obey Christ the Lawgiver. And when we try to obey Christ the Lawgiver but fall short, we will repair to Christ the Savior who will give us the strength to face Christ the Lawgiver again and more successfully.

Chapter 11

The Eighth Commandment

"Thou shalt not steal" (Exodus 20:15).

John Ruskin wrote that "the law of nature is that a certain quantity of work is necessary to produce a certain quantity of good. If you want knowledge, you must toil for it; if food, you must toil for it; if pleasure, you must toil for it." The person who does not do this certain amount of work, but learns or eats or enjoys himself, is a thief, unless he is rich by inheritance, in which case someone in his line did the necessary quantity of work. If a person gets the good things of life in any other way than by earning them, by necessary charity, or by fortunate inheritance, he is a thief. An honest man is, by definition, a person who accepts only what he has earned by his labors.

Let us apply this principle to gambling. What is gambling? Everybody knows what gambling is, you say. We think not. We believe that if people really knew what gambling was, gambling would no longer exist. Deliberately to arrange things so that huge wealth is offered for no good reason, and earned by nothing but luck, needs only to be stated in order to be condemned by all right-minded observers. Yet that is what gambling amounts to. It has been more briefly defined by Johnson as "the mode of transferring property without any intermediate good."

A man would be put in jail for taking property in that way, or put in an asylum for giving property in that way, through any mode other than gambling. That is why the original meaning of the word "gambler" was "false gamester," or one who played an unfair game. Aristotle lumped thieves and gamblers together. The Word of God condemned gambling roundly: "But you who forsake the Lord, who forget My holy mountain, who set a table for Fortune and fill cups of mixed wine for Destiny" (Isaiah 65:11). The early Christian Church forbade it, and even viewed it as grounds for excommunication. The church father Tertullian bluntly stated that a gambler was not a Christian and a Christian would not be a gambler. In the opinion of most Christians through the ages, gambling qualifies as a violation of the eighth commandment: "Thou shalt not steal."

Gambling is not only bad in itself; it is worse in its effects. As the poet said:

> This is the very curse of evil deed,
> That of new evil it becomes the seed.

This could have been written especially about gambling. Here, for example, are a few statistics for England between 1895 and 1907. Please remember that these are only the cases that were recorded; informed imagination could multiply these numbers many times. As a result of gambling there were 156 suicides or attempted suicides; 719 thefts or embezzlements; and 442 bankruptcies.

Scotland tells the same story. Its National League Against Betting and Gambling says, "The exploitation of the nation's nitwits by the unscrupulous gambling interests is a prominent factor in the nation's apostasy from religion, in the collapse of conscience, in the loss of moral values, in the growing dishonesty and lack of truthfulness and moral insensibility in the land."

What of the gamblingest nation in the world? Well, we are still great. Why? Because we have not yet completely lost the heritage which made us great. What was that? Honest work for an honest dollar; the dignity of human toil; respect for fellow man; fear of God. But the new craze for gambling is sapping our foundations. Like the scion of a wealthy family, we are betting our inheritance away. We are on the down side of the old cycle: discipline produces wealth, but wealth tends to undermine the discipline that produced it. Gambling is undisciplined living. It is an enemy of society, and a friend to criminals. It is the keystone in the arch of the underworld. Drunkenness, robberies, prostitution, political corruption, drug addiction, murder—the whole empire rests on gambling. It is as if the devil had said, "Upon *this* rock, I will build *my* kingdom."

The same principle of honest work applies to business. Bradstreet once investigated bankruptcies in the United States over a period of two years and found that only 20 percent of these failures had resulted from legitimate causes or undue competition. The other 80 percent were due to dishonesty or incompetence. Dishonesty, the path to the fast buck, may seem to offer great advantage in advancing one's interest, but in the long run it does not seem to work out that way. If we consider the really long run—the eternal run, if you please—we know that it never works out to anything but the thief's ruin.

One may also incur a violation of the eighth commandment by not paying debts. Notice that one person may take money from another's pocket without lifting his

wallet. For example, if you owe money to another and do
not pay it when you are able to do so, are you not stealing just as surely as if you had reached into his pocket? If
you owe him the money, it is his money, not yours. If
you keep it when you could repay it, are you not keeping
his money? If you spend it on something else, are you
not spending his money? You may say that you need
such and such, and therefore you will delay the promised
payment. What difference is there between doing that and
saying to yourself, "I need such and such but do not
have the money to buy it, so I will steal my neighbor's
money in order to get it?" Using money that belongs to
someone else is stealing, no matter how you came to have
the money in the first place. Of course, lending companies
make you pay for your theft.

Some are impressed by the fact that some dishonest
persons do prosper, at least for a while, in this world.
Does not even the Psalmist, man of God that he was, feel
vexed about the wicked who prosper as the green bay
tree (Psalm 37:35)? Does Christ not tell of the fool who,
though foolish in not taking consideration for his soul,
nonetheless was able to build bigger and bigger barns
until his soul was demanded of him? There are those who
wonder if the universe really is on the side of the honest
when inequities so prevail in this world.

Let us speak to this moral problem of the supposed
prosperity of the wicked. In the first place, do the wicked
have any real prosperity? Granted, they may have much
of this world's goods. If they get them dishonestly, do
they get any benefits? Obviously they do. They can buy
more and better food, clothing, dwellings. By their
money, therefore, dishonest men may live a bigger and
better animal existence.

Is that an advantage for a man? Not in itself, you say, but as a means to an end. Very well, to what end do these things lead? To God? Definitely not, for we are speaking of wicked men, who defy God and His laws and who become prosperous by disregarding God. If they do not gain God by defying Him, what end do they gain? Moral and spiritual pleasures? There can be no moral and spiritual pleasures if God is alienated. Intellectual pleasures? Yes, they can buy more and better books, attend superior lectures, perhaps associate with more dilettantes, patronize the arts. But can there be any mental rest for the wicked? If all intellectual roads lead to God, who made us in His image and endowed us with our superior mentality, what can this wicked person's intellectual pursuits be but blind alleys? Is this knowledge, or is it not what Paul calls the "reprobate mind" of those who would not have God in their thinking (Romans 1:28)? They have the tools of thought and they use them, but all for the purpose of not having God in their thinking. What is this but an intellectual prodigal in a far country, reduced to eating intellectual swine's fare? I repeat, is this knowledge, or is it not the behavior of those "ever learning and never able to come to the knowledge of the truth" (1 Timothy 3:7)?

So I ask, what does the wicked person have? He has money which has increased his material comforts. He is better able to live in an animal sense, but at the price of forfeiting his mind, his soul, and his conscience. When described in this way, even to the man of this world who is interested in making a profit however he can, is this a profitable transaction? Can he call this a fair return on his investment of time and effort? Really now, "What does it profit a man if he gain the whole world and lose his own soul?" (Matthew 16:26).

In the second place, consider the positive liabilities. We have just noted the negative ones: what such a person does not have, and the uselessness of what he does have. But notice also the debits he suffers. There is his restless mind, for example. Nothing but God answers the questions of origins, destiny, and purpose. The man may search elsewhere, but he is like a thirsty man in the desert, who cannot stop seeking though every step is torture. If he says that there is no God, no moral law, no conscience, will his mind let him off with that assertion? Is he sure he is right? Does he know with certainty that there is no God? Can he prove his atheism beyond the shadow of a doubt? But as long as there is even the shadow of a doubt, how can there be anything but torment in his mind? Suppose he is wrong; suppose death comes and an angry God immediately meets him to take account of his unbelief and defiance. He does not believe this will happen, but he does not know for sure. Unless he has sound reason for certain assurance that there is no God, no judgment, no hell, what peace can there be in his mind?

Third, there is the evidence that his worst fears are justified. He may not know or believe this evidence. But nevertheless there *is* evidence that God is true and that judgment will come. So some day, when his animal comforts are over and he appears before his Judge to be judged for the deeds done in the flesh, he will wish immediately that he had never spurned the love and the law of God. One moment in hell will convince him forever that his whole life was one awful mistake. He will gladly exchange all the joys he ever knew in this world to have one minute of the wrath of God removed from him.

The fourth factor that makes the way of the transgres-

sor (the so-called prosperous transgressor) harder is the
simple fact that the happiest persons are those who walk
the straight and narrow way, who despise the profit of
this world, who would forfeit their life rather than compromise their integrity one whit. Not only do the righteous realize that "a small thing which the righteous hath
is better than great riches of the ungodly," but the ungodly realize it dimly too. In accumulating all their treasures on earth, they have not achieved blessedness, while
those poor godly folk, with a disdain for all that this world
offers, have more than all the riches this world can afford.
The wicked may not be able to understand this clearly,
but they know, when they become acquainted with one
godly person, that he has found, without seeking for it,
what they cannot find by their most relentless pursuit:
happiness. This only aggravates the worldlings' sense of
their futility and folly and makes their cup all the more
bitter. For the godly, the truth is still the same: he who
has God and nothing else has as much as he who has God
and the whole world besides.

A special word to students, for whom I have a particular concern. If you are tempted to cheat, it is for some
presumed advantage you hope to secure thereby.
Granted, you may achieve that supposed advantage. You
may pass the course that you should have flunked. You
may receive a stolen diploma. You may then get a job on
false pretense of knowing some things which you do not
know. Is this really an advantage? What will it profit if
you to gain a world of diplomas while forfeiting your own
soul, disturbing your conscience, and making an enemy
of God? Is this good business? Is this a profitable bar-
gain?

But remember, you who cooperate with those who

cheat, that you are cheaters too. Those who aid and abet crimes are themselves regarded as criminals by the law. Granted that there is a difference between the active and the passive criminal—between the one who initiates an act of wrongdoing and the one who simply does not resist it—the fact remains that each one is essential to perpetrating it. If it is clear that a person who sees a murder in process and is able to prevent it but does not do so bears part of the guilt for the murder, is the point not equally clear with respect to the sin of stealing?

Anyone, therefore, who values his own body, soul, and spirit will not play free and loose with the eighth commandment. If he steals anything at all, however, small, he steals from God, because all things are God's. And since God forbids him to steal, he buys the world at the cost of antagonizing God.

"Will ye rob God?" asks the prophet Malachi. He was referring to the act of withholding from God that portion of our money which is required as a token that all we possess belongs to Him. If all we possess belongs to God, does not the very supposition that there is such a thing as "our money" make thieves of us? If we spend anything we have without a sense of our stewardship to God, to whom we must some day give an account for all the deeds done in the body, are we not acting as if something were ours which is not? That is, are we not stealing, and stealing from God? And if this is true of our money, is it not equally true of our time, of all we possess, indeed of our very lives? Therefore, the person who does not endeavor to worship God with all his heart, soul, mind, and strength—with everything he possesses, at all times and under all circumstances—is a thief.

Chapter 12

The Ninth Commandment

"Thou shalt not bear false witness against thy neighbor" (Exodus 20:16).

This is, for us, the most difficult of the ten commandments to interpret. Nevertheless, we feel that a sound understanding of our obligation in this area may be obtained.

Let us begin with a miscellaneous assortment of situations involving this principle. In the army, soldiers fighting in the South Pacific used to wear clothes designed to blend with their jungle environment, in such a way that the enemy would think no soldiers were there when actually they were there, ready to attack. This was calculated deception.

Another illustration: a man once admitted that he had stolen a piece of rope, but neglected to mention that there had been a horse attached to one end of it. Was that a lie?

That form of literature which we call fiction represents many things as having happened which did not actually take place but were merely imagined by the writer. Is that misrepresentation or lying?

A man pursued by gangsters takes refuge in another man's house, where the gangsters come in search of him. When they ask the owner of the house if the fugitive is inside and he answers "No," is that bearing false witness in the sense of this commandment?

Pharaoh had said that all Hebrew male children should be delivered to him in order to be put to death. When the midwives who spirited them away explained that the Hebrew mothers were lively and that the children were delivered before they (the midwives) could arrive, were they acting rightly or wrongly?

A person calls on a friend to visit, and the maid says "She is not at home" even though she is upstairs. What of that?

When people leave home for a vacation, they often leave a light burning to give any would-be thieves the impression that they are still at home. Is this honest? Are they playing fair with the crooks?

A student once asked to be excused for absence from class, saying he had been "indisposed." What he meant was not that he had been ill, but that he was indisposed to come to class. How about that?

In football, a halfback bends over, pretending to run with the ball, while the quarterback is dropping back to throw the real ball. Or what of the feint in boxing? We could go on, but perhaps we have covered the field of typical instances that raise the great questions about the ninth commandment.

Some of these instances are easily eliminated from classification as "lies" in the evil sense of that word, or as violations of this commandment. For example, we all immediately sense that the soldier's camouflage, writing fiction, and athletic fakes are not lies. Not only do we not condemn a halfback who has two men tackling him while his teammate runs the other way with the ball, but we make an All-American of him if he does it often enough. If a novelist makes our blood boil or our tears flow over totally imaginary situations, we give him a literary prize.

Why is this? Why do men instinctively recognize that there is no evil in these forms of deliberate deception? Because they are not really deceptions at all. In all these instances we know from the very beginning that we are playing a game in which the rules are different from those of ordinary life. It is understood in advance that the army will try to hide its presence from the enemy, that a half-back will try to fool his tacklers, and that the novel is fiction. We are not deceived.

So it would seem that, for a lie to be a lie, it would have to be supposed to be the truth. Or, more exactly, the person who tells or acts out this deception must be intending to deceive. To clarify further, a person is committing deception if he does so in an overall situation in which it is understood that he will not deceive—where it is assumed that he will speak and act truly. Deception under these circumstances (which we may call "normal" circumstances) would be a lie and a violation of the commandment.

Let us turn to some of the other instances. What about the man and the rope? What he told was certainly the truth: he stole a rope. Nor did he tell any falsehood. He did not say that he had not stolen a horse. Was he guilty, then, of telling a lie when he did not state anything false? It depends on whether he had any obligation to tell the whole truth, or whether what he said purported to be the whole truth. If he had an obligation to tell the whole truth, and if he mentioned the rope but neglected to mention the horse, he was lying. Or, even if he had no such obligation but nonetheless told his story in such a way as to give his hearers the impression that all he stole was a rope, he would also be bearing false witness. Of course (if he were exceptionally stupid), he might not have realized that people would be misled by such a representation. In that case, he would still have told what amounted to a lie, but without being a liar. Intention is one necessary component of a liar, just as it is of a murderer, thief, and profaner.

What of the light in the vacant house which says people are there who are not, and of the maid who says someone is not home who is? The first instance is clearly intentional deception. The question is whether one owes a potential thief any more truthfulness than he owes an enemy in war. If it is legitimate to place rubber tanks so as to fool enemy bombers into targeting them, may we not also mislead thieves who are enemies of society? Let us hold off on this point until we come to the fugitive.

As for the maid—can her visitor also be regarded as an enemy of society who does not deserve normal treatment? Hardly, unless that visitor were a criminal of some sort, intending to commit harm, in which case this would fall in the fugitive category. But is this a proper answer for normal persons? Perhaps—if it can be truly said, as some maintain, that when a lady states through a maid that she is not home, this does not, according to the language of etiquette, actually mean that she is not bodily present in the house at that time, but that she is not socially accessible to this would-be visitor. It is conceivable that this is the understood meaning of the expression in many circles. In such a case, this would not be a question of honesty but of tact, courtesy, or kindness. Otherwise, it would be intentional deception under perfectly normal circumstances that allow for no justifiable misrepresentation.

What about the "indisposed" student? Here there can be no doubt that this expression has no esoteric meaning, such as the expression "She is not home" may have. While the word itself is ambiguous and could, in some other context, mean a psychological indisposition, that meaning is not possible in this instance. If the professor understood the reference to psychological rather than physical indisposition to come to class, he would not accept the excuse. For the excuse to be acceptable, the professor must understand it as referring to physical indisposition, and the student offering the excuse would be fully aware of that. So, if he was hoping to have the excuse accepted, he would at the same time be hoping to succeed in deceiving his professor.

But what of the person fleeing from murderers and hiding in a house whose owner denies his presence? This is a flat lie. The man says he is not there, while knowing very well that he is there. He intends deceit, desiring that the murderers be diverted and the fugitive saved. There can be no question about the meaning of the language; the question here is about obligation. Does a person in such circumstances have any obligation to tell the truth? I would propose that this situation is not any different from the war scenario. A warring enemy and a murderer are alike enemies of the state and society. They lie, deceive, and kill. Does society owe them any advantages? I think not. They have no right to assistance, cooperation, information or anything other than to be apprehended and punished. It would seem that, under such circumstances, it would be a person's *duty* to deceive deliberately, with the hope and prayer that his deception would succeed. But again, that is because this is not a normal situation. Just as there are other situations, such as games and war, in which it is understood that the usual rules of honesty are waived, it is also understood that murderers have no right to truthful information which would help them commit their crime.

Someone will ask whether Christians on trial for their lives were justified in pretending to recant. After all, it is generally acknowledged that men should not persecute others for their religious beliefs, and certainly not for believing what is true. If Christianity is the revelation of God, the person who persecutes a believer is fighting against God. Under such circumstances, would a person not be justified in lying to save his life? Is this situation similar to a condition of war or an escape from gangsters? If lying is justified in those cases, why not in this similar one?

If this is the case, we note in passing, then martyrdom was one grand mistake, and those whom we celebrate as heroes of the faith were actually fools. We could still admire their devotion, but we would have to classify it as fanaticism rather than courage. These consequences we must face if this proposed judgment be true. Nor dare we shrink from this interpretation simply because it would compel us to revise our judgments at many points.

There is, however, one key difference between this situation and the others cited. Here it is the duly constituted government which has put the person on trial. It has the legitimate privilege of asking its citizens about anything which it considers of concern to the state's welfare. The citizen owes respect and obedience to his government. He is asked to support, honor, and pray for it. He cannot refuse his cooperation by lying to it. Granted, the government should not make mistakes, such as killing innocent persons. But it does make mistakes at times, and the true citizen, while attempting to point them out, will not reject the government as such because it does make mistakes. Doing so would be to overthrow the authorities ordained by God, as we have intimated in discussing the fifth commandment.

A mistaken government is not tantamount to an enemy of the state or the individual. No true citizen can so regard it. He must, therefore, respect it and tell it the truth it wants to know. If the government mistakenly insists, thinking this is in the state's welfare, that it is necessary to put these citizens to death, they must be prepared to die—with love for God and honor toward the men whom God has appointed to this office.

Let us try to formulate some sort of definition of this difficult concept of lying. We will define lying as the deliberate and conscious falsification of facts, either by misrepresentation or partial representation, when normal conditions are prevailing and there is an obligation to speak all or some of the truth. This definition rules out those misrepresentations made under abnormal conditions, such as play, war, and fiction. It also rules out unintentional mistakes. At the same time it will rule in those misrepresentations which consist of misleading use of words or expressions. It also indicates the mendacity of partial representation on some occasions.

So a person may lie in many different ways. He may tell a falsehood by mentioning the truth that he has stolen a rope; that is, he can tell a lie by not telling all the truth. In some cases one may tell a pernicious lie by saying nothing at all. If one is asked to testify in court against gangsterdom, and fear of retaliation shuts his mouth and he gets what is called "underworld lockjaw," he is lying. To be sure, he is lying in order to save his life, but that does not change the fact that he is lying. And if the preservation of our lives, as we have already shown, could ever justify the neglect of duty, then the moral order is destroyed, because our lives are more or less at stake all the time in every duty. We must hate our lives if we would be disciples of Christ who is the upholder of the moral code.

The forms of lying just mentioned were negative ones; that is, they consisted in not saying or doing certain things. There are also many positive forms of lying. A misleading action can tell a lie as clearly as a word. When a parent tells his child that it is good for people to go to church and then he himself does not attend, his actions tell a lie. They say that it is *not* good for persons to go to church.

Equivocation, or double talk, is another form of lying, as illustrated by our "indisposed" student. A person may speak "tongue in cheek," not really meaning to say what the words seem, when properly interpreted in their context, to say. Perhaps this liar could not be convicted in any human court, at least not if he had a sufficiently shrewd lawyer; but the court of God will not hold him guiltless of violating the ninth commandment.

So there are many forms of lying in addition to the outright misstatement. The bald lie, in fact, is probably seldom told. Professed religious people will certainly be on the alert against gross violations of this commandment; they must also be aware of the subtle evasions of this duty. Once again, the only way to fulfill the commandment forbidding lying is by consistently doing and saying the truth. If we cultivate honesty, we leave no room for deception. An honest man cannot, morally speaking, break the ninth commandment. In the last analysis, there is no way to avoid breaking it but by being thoroughly honest, inwardly and outwardly, before man as well as

God, in obviously moral situations and those not so obvious, in school, in business, in our homes and outside
them, in church and on the street, here and there, everywhere. It has been well said that an honest man is the
noblest work of God.

Chapter 13

The Tenth Commandment

"Thou shalt not covet thy neighbor's house, thou shalt not covet thy neighbor's wife, nor his manservant, nor his maidservant, nor his ox, nor his ass, nor anything that is thy neighbor's" (Exodus 20:17).

If the traditional ethic of religion is an opiate to the people, as Communism has charged, it is when teaching this tenth commandment, "Thou shalt not covet." The tenth commandment goes further than the eighth, forbidding nor merely the taking of a neighbor's property but even the desire to take it. And if coveting is a mortal sin, the only way to avoid it is to be content with what one has.

Since this moral law exists in the midst of gross inequities and extremely uneven distribution of wealth, it does afford tremendous confirmation to the status quo. Communism has rightly noticed that religion is an opiate; that is, it tends to make men satisfied with things as they are. We have several things to observe at this point, but first of all, let us note that this objection is not really directed against religion as such, but against the moral code of men and nations. Nor is it aimed at the specially revealed moral code alone, for this is part of natural revelation as well.

Second, if satisfaction with our lot, whatever it may be, is not inculcated—if there is not this "opiate"—then

the alternative must necessarily be uninterrupted dissat-
isfaction and frustration. The world never has been and
never will be ordered to everyone's satisfaction.
Communism cannot hope to satisfy everyone either. It
too must have its hierarchy, for example. Some must be
the thinkers, writers, organizers, and rulers, while others
will desire these jobs and not receive them. If they continue to covet what they do not have, they will be miserable and frustrated, in the very bosom of a Communist
state. No one will contend that it is good for men to be in
a state of constant frustration. Indeed, doctors prescribe
opiates for people if that is the only way to relieve their
futile tensions.

Third, a man is of no great value to anyone else when
he is unhappy himself. Being preoccupied with his own
misery, he has little room for concern for others. If this
frustration cannot be conquered, he will spread his
frustration to others. In other words, if coveting were not
restrained this world would become a veritable hell for
everyone.

Fourth, contentment is not really an opiate. An opiate
is something that makes a person insensitive to his condition. Contentment does not make a person insensitive
to his condition, but rather makes him more sensitive to
it. He is not contented because he now thinks this is an
ideal world, in which everything is as it ought to be and
there is no room for betterment. That conception would
indeed be an opiate. But this Pollyanna view is not the
doctrine of religion. Religion teaches that there are sin,
maladjustment, and judgment in this world. The believer
prays for God's kingdom to come and His will to be done,
on earth as it is done in heaven. His very association with
God makes him realize more keenly the great discrepancy

between what this world is and what it ought to be.

No, his contentment is at another point. He knows that all things, even the evil things, work together for good. He is not content with evil, or he would not pray for the coming of the Kingdom. He is content with the plan and program of God, which are tending toward an ultimate good end, the mere contemplation of which gives the believer great contentment. In other words, contentment does not require a person to see this world other than as it is, but to see the plan of God, which is not apparent on the surface of things but which is open to the eye of faith.

In fact, contentment with the will and plan of God leads a person to struggle for reform. It has the opposite of an enervating effect; it has an energizing effect. This contentment rests on assurance of God's plan, which calls for the introduction of God's kingdom and which involves the believer in activity on behalf of that kingdom. Everything which is inconsistent with that goal he will strive to correct, and everything which is in accord with it he will attempt to bolster and advance. While he knows he will be frustrated in his efforts to some degree, he also knows that God will grant as much success as God in His wisdom sees fit to grant.

What God does not yet grant, the Christian will acquiesce in, even as he continues, at every opportunity, to rectify the situation. This makes it possible, necessary, and natural for him to be a happy warrior, a confident reformer, and a conqueror in the midst of defeats. Even the defeats are victories for him, since he knows that they too are parts of God's ultimate purpose. Thus the contented, noncovetous person strives constantly and relentlessly, abounding in the Lord's work and not growing weary in well-doing. At the same time, because of his humility and patience with God and the divine purposes, the frustrations God permits do not frustrate him.

The Communist thinks that religion promises "pie in the sky, by and by" and that this promise keeps people satisfied with unsatisfactory conditions in the here-and-now. It is true that religion does promise, to those who walk by faith, that they shall some day be with God in unbroken communion forever. There will indeed be pie in the sky, by and by. And there is no doubt that this promise greatly encourages any believer to endure with assurance any adversity in this fleeting world. But it does more than produce endurance; it produces joy. It is not possible for a person to rest assured of eternal felicity and not be happy now at that prospect. Moreover, religion affords real and present spiritual joys, such as a peace that this world cannot know. So the notion that the hope of joy hereafter enables the follower of true religion to endure misery for a few decades here misses the point. The point is not that this future hope enables a person to "grin and bear it" for now—though it can indeed provide that strength—and certainly not that it teaches resignation to things as they are. However, believers also know a present joy that is more real and wonderful than any amount of earthly possessions, held privately or in common, could ever yield.

We might summarize this point by saying that religion does not merely promise pie in the sky, by and by, and nothing in this present world. On the contrary, it promises pie here and now and, in the by-and-by, pie with ice cream.

The tenth commandment shows something of the innerness of the law. It is more apparent, on the very sur-

face of this law, than in the other commandments that a
right disposition of the heart is essential to its observance. Christ had to remind His generation that the sixth
commandment forbade unjustifiable anger and that the
seventh commandment forbade lust as well as overt adultery; but it was not necessary to point out the inward aim
of the tenth commandment. This one is directed immediately at the heart and never goes beyond that.

"Thou shalt not covet." If a man has this illicit desire,
he has transgressed this commandment. "Thou shalt not
covet thy neighbor's wife." He does not have to take her
or marry her or abuse her, but simply covet her and he
has broken the law. In a certain sense, when Christ says
that whoever looks on a woman to lust after her has already committed adultery in his heart, this means that the
person has broken the tenth as well as the seventh commandment. Coveting the neighbor's wife is adultery.
Likewise, coveting his goods is stealing.

Coveting has two "built-in" liabilities connected with
it—that is, consequences which naturally flow from it.
These features are distinct from the explicit threat that
God Himself will directly punish the violator of His law.
God has also ordered things in such a way that His own
disapproval will be apparent in the consequences of evil
acts. This is not the most important part of the truth regarding judgment; that is, these built-in liabilities connected with coveting are as nothing when compared with
the ultimate wrath of God. For example, if a person en-
gages in sexual promiscuity he may contract some sort of
disease, but that pales in comparison to the judgment of
hell which God assures the adulterer is to be his portion
forever. Those people who think the saying "the wages of
sin is death" means only that sin tends toward death in

the natural order miss this more important, eternal aspect of the truth. Nevertheless, the consequences of sin experienced in this world are still something in themselves, as they show how the moral wind blows; that is, they intimate that the author of our universe is opposed to this way of behaving and that they should prepare to meet their God some day for a personal accounting.

The first of these built-in liabilities is that coveting makes for war and destruction. How could it be otherwise? If I desire what someone else has and it is legitimate for me to do so, then it is also legitimate for me to satisfy my desire. But that involves taking the item I covet from him who has it. He, however, is not disposed to let me have what it his. He wants it too, and it belongs to him. His objections mean nothing to me; I desire it, I must have it, and it is legitimate for me to take it. But if the other man thinks it is legitimate not to let me take it, the outcome is obvious: one or both of the combatants will be killed. For if that covetousness if permitted to burn, it must be satisfied, destroyed, or confined. As a matter of fact, this is what lies at the base of most, if not all, crime, war, bloodshed, and the various inhumanities man commits against man.

There is a one-act play which presents vividly this destructive power of coveting. It deals with two men, each of whom has a possession which the other needs. One man has water on his land and the other has jewels. Each man covets the other's possession. Neither one will give his item first for fear that the other will then renege on his part of the deal. Not trusting each other, they strike a compromise. While the one man holds the cup to the other's lips, the latter puts a necklace about the former's neck. The play concludes with the two men dying, one from strangulation and the other from poisoning.

Beyond this destructive antisocial tendency, the other liability of coveting is its sheer futility. Beyond all the rivalry, war, and social unrest that arise from coveting, if we consider the individual alone we find that this coveting does him no good either. Christ put it this way: "Life consists not in the abundance of things possessed" (Luke 12:15).

Tolstoy wrote a play called *Enough*, the story of a man who was to have all the land he could traverse in a given period of time. The man died trying for the utmost, because "enough" proved to be an elusive concept. Even if men could get what they covet, they would not be happy; they would always covet something else. When Alexander had the world, he then coveted more worlds to conquer.

Man's heart is restless till it finds its rest in God. There is no resting place in this world or in anything it contains. Godliness with contentment is great gain, but all gain without godly contentment is frustration. Coveting is a fire; the more you feed it, the more it burns. It is not assuaged when fed, but only demands more. So the more a person's coveting is satisfied, the more it is unsatisfied. The more he gets, the more he wants. Coveting grows larger and larger with every satisfaction, and in the end the person is more miserable than at the beginning. If he succeeds, he fails; if he gets what he wants, he still wants more than he gets. He drives out one devil of desire, as it were, by paying him off with gratification, and then seven more come in its place.

Life consists not in the abundance of things possessed. Indeed, the more abundance one has to satisfy his coveting, the less life he has.

Coveting is such a disease that, while it is unsatisfied

in any one particular, it destroys all health of soul. This can be seen, for example, in the story of Haman, in the Old Testament book of Esther, who was of highest rank under the king of Persia. He had everything, we would say. But not quite everything. He did not have the show of obeisance by one Jew named Mordecai. This was irritating, to be sure, but should this have destroyed his vast prestige, power, and pleasure? It should not have, but it did. Haman had no peace because of this Mordecai. He lay awake thinking of ways to make Mordecai bow or to destroy him. His desires raged and all else was forgotten. There was no comfort for Haman while this Jew lived.

Ultimately Haman himself was destroyed in his attempt to destroy Mordecai, but before that happened he had already been destroyed by his covetousness. Thus we see, and how well we know from our own experience, that one thing coveted can occupy our attention to the detriment of everything we possess and enjoy. Coveting is the camel which, once it has its nose in the tent, will surely push the owner out.

Part 3

Supernaturally Revealed
Moral Laws

Chapter 14

Repentance

First among the duties of the unconverted or of men in general, let us consider repentance and restitution. God, says Paul, calls all men everywhere to repent (Acts 17:30). "Except ye repent, said Jesus, "ye shall all likewise perish" (Luke 13:3, 5). "Repent, and be baptized every one of you in the name of Jesus Christ for the remission of sins, and ye shall receive the gift of the Holy Ghost" (Acts 2:38).

The word for repentance is *metanoiein*, which means to change the mind. In what respects men are called upon to change their mind is not immediately evident, but it becomes plain as the biblical message is appreciated. Men are by nature enemies of God (Romans 5:8), and the carnal mind is at enmity against God and is not subject to the law; neither, indeed, can it be (Romans 8:7). The thoughts or intents of the mind are only evil continually (Genesis 6:5). The natural man (or unconverted man) does not understand the things of God (1 Corinthians 2:14). Thus we learn that the mind of man which must be changed is a mind hostile to God and His law. The change must signify a becoming friendly or receptive to the law of God and to God as its Author.

This inner change—for a change of mind is an inner and not an external change—will have certain outward expressions which issue from it. Since it is a change from friendliness to hostility toward sin, it will be manifested in the repudiation of all vices formerly practiced. No sin of commission or omission will escape its universal sweep. The mind is now opposed to every manifestation of evil. While this change is most directly related to God, in that one now abhors and turns from what God abhors, it is also related to man. Thus the person loathes his former dishonesties, unkindnesses, and cruelties toward other men and seeks to rectify these, through what is called restitution.

A tremendous ethical problem arises at this point. If a man is naturally at enmity with God, if his mind cannot be subject to God, if his very nature is hostile to God—how can he change his mind? How can he repent? It would seem, from the very nature of the case, that he cannot. This inference regarding the nature of man, in his present condition, is confirmed by Scripture. Christ says that he who commits sin is the bondservant of sin (John 8:34). A corrupt tree cannot bring forth good fruit (Matthew 7:18). The prophet says that men cannot change their sinful hearts any more than an Ethiopian can change his skin or a leopard his spots. Paul says that men are dead in trespasses and sin (Ephesians 2:1).

The great ethicist Immanuel Kant and many others have argued that "I ought" necessarily implies "I can." Where responsibility exists there must be ability. If a man has an obligation to do anything, he must have the power to do it. On the other hand, if he is unable to do something, neither is he responsible; he cannot be held accountable for not doing it. How can a person be blamed for not doing something which he could not do? Kant felt that the very existence of a categorical imperative, a law of ought, required the postulate of freedom, not bondage.

The vast majority of mankind would concur with these concepts, at least in part. But suppose a person who is able to act virtuously begins to act sinfully. Is it possible for him to habituate himself to sinful action so that, in time, he will be unable to act virtuously? We will not yet settle whether it is possible for a person to fall into such a condition of bondage, but for now we will simply ask whether, if he did, he would still be responsible. That is, if a person had so habituated himself to wrongdoing that he was no longer capable of doing right, would he remain responsible for doing right? Or would he be no longer responsible for doing right as soon as he reached the point where he could not do right any more?

Probably no rational person would say that if a person did wrong so consistently that he lost his ability to do right, he would therefore be absolved of all future responsibility. We would hesitate to say any such thing, for this would reward violators of the law with freedom from the law. By the reverse reasoning, those who kept the law, if they became more able to do so by observing the practice of keeping it, would be penalized by becoming more and more obliged to it. The moral law would become more exacting as a person conformed to it and less exacting as a person rebelled against it. The more a person respected the law, the more it would require of him, the more he disregarded it the more he would be free from its authority. This would be a strange moral world indeed. As far as we know, no one has ever considered the moral world to be like this, but exactly the opposite.

But then we must admit that if a person could disobey the law of God so constantly that he became incapable of obeying it, he would not therefore cease to be obligated to it. He would be responsible though not able. He would owe the law its demands even though he was no longer able to pay them. He would be incapable of repentance, but would be called to it nonetheless. If this is so, then there are at least some circumstances where responsibility does not assume ability—cases where the existence of the categorical imperative does not at all imply freedom to fulfill moral commands. There may be other situations, such as inherited guilt, which could cause inability without the loss of responsibility.

So we return to our question: is it possible for a person who originally has power to do a certain moral act to reach the point, through immoral action, where he no longer can do that moral act? Let us try to find the answer to this question in reference to some specific duty. Let us consider the duty to love God with all our heart, mind, soul, and strength. There is no question that this is our duty. It is equally certain that we do not fulfill this duty. But are we *able* to fulfill it? Yes, in one sense: we possess the heart and mind that could be used in loving God. We have the necessary faculties and powers.

But that is a rather lame and obvious observation. The real question is, do we have the *disposition* to use our heart and mind this way? We do not love in this way. But are we disposed to do so? Who would say that he is so disposed—that he has the subjective ability to love God with all his heart? Who would not rather confess that he does not find within him the necessary inclination to respond to this command? In that sense of the word we must admit that we are not able to love God with all our heart and mind. At the same time we recognize that this inability which we feel is not native to us. It does not belong to our humanity as such. It is an extraneous factor; it is not, in the ultimate sense, natural. For what would be more natural for a creature than to love his Creator with all his creaturely faculties?

So, then, we seem to have evidence that it is possible for a person to have had a native ability which he has somehow lost. Yet at the same time our sense of obligation to love God is not diminished but, on the contrary, heightened because of our rebellion.

But all this has been pure speculation. Let us repair to revelation itself for further light. The Bible not only confirms what has been discovered independently of it, but it shows exactly how this inability has come about (see especially Genesis 3 and Romans 5:12–21). It confirms our sense that this condition is not natural. It teaches that we were not made this way. God did not create us in our present image. Rather, these passages tell us that we were originally created in His moral image of knowledge, righteousness, and holiness. The forefather of our race underwent probation for all, and by his disobedience to divine command all his posterity sinned and fell with him. While the natural image of God (our faculties) and our dominion over the creatures survived the Fall, the goodness of His nature was lost. The lamp remained, but the oil was gone. This is when man died spiritually, so that Paul later describes us, "You hath He quickened, who were dead in trespasses and sins" (Ephesians 2:1). He who sins is the bondservant of sin, and from this wretched condition all Christians are obliged to turn in grief and hatred of their sin—that is, in repentance.

This excursion has only succeeded in heightening our dilemma. We are independently obliged to repent, and yet we do not have the inclination, disposition, subjective ability, or whatever you wish to call it (as long as you do not forget that we still do have all the faculties and light necessary, that is, all the objective ability necessary). But why does God call us to a duty we no longer can perform, indeed one we have never been able to perform? When we as a race were sound morally, we did not need to repent, and when we fell into unsoundness we could not repent. So when we were able, it was not necessary, and when it became necessary we were no longer able. Why, then, does God ask the impossible?

First, He probably intends by this command to show us our inability. Where there is no law, there is no sin. If we did not have any duty, we would never know our inability to perform duty. But when God tells us that our whole pattern of thought and life is enmity against Him and that we are hell-bent for destruction; there He warns us that unless we repent we shall perish, and yet we find that we are unable to repent, and that so desperate is our situation that when a remedy (repentance) is offered we are too weak to take it—then we know beyond all question how undone we are. It may seem bad enough to be a wicked person, but how much worse to be so wicked that you are no longer able to be otherwise!

Second, this inability accentuates the sovereignty of God. It becomes apparent that if we are unable to deliver ourselves, or even put ourselves in a position where God may deliver us, then we depend on God entirely. We need Him not only to pardon us, but to give us the inclination to seek His pardon. He must be indeed the author as well as the finisher of our salvation; the provider and the applier; the one who provides the life-giving water and also the one who brings us to the water to drink. No longer are we the vaunted captains of our souls, masters of our fate, but rather we are utter slaves in chains, and our only hope is a "peradventure" of God. It is God who gives repentance, and He does so only as He chooses to do so (Romans 9:18). Augustine realized this dilemma when he uttered the great and oft-quoted words, "Lord, give what You command and then command what You will." In the metrical version of Psalm 51 we read these words:

> I am evil born in sin
> Thou desirest truth within

And from that cry of despair come these words following:

> Thou alone my Savior art
> Teach Thy wisdom to my heart.

A third purpose in God's commanding men to repent who are, of themselves, unable to do so is to set them seeking for the grace of God. This has been sufficiently discussed in chapter 2, when we dealt with sanctions, and we need not rehearse it here.

Chapter 15

Faith

Another ethical duty taught by Christianity and required of all men is faith. "This is life eternal, that they know Thee the only true God, and Jesus Christ, whom Thou hast sent" (John 17:3). This "know" is more than mere speculative exercise but includes acceptance and communion; that is, it involves faith. Likewise, in the same gospel it is written, "He came unto His own, and His own received Him not. But as many as received Him, to them gave He the authority to become the sons of God, who were born not of the will of man nor of the will of the flesh, but of God" (John 1:11–13). "Believe on the Lord Jesus Christ, and thou shalt be saved," declared Paul (Acts 16:31). The world by its wisdom did not know God. "I am not ashamed of the gospel of Christ: for it is the power of God unto salvation to everyone that believeth; to the Jew first, and also the Greek. For therein is the righteousness of God revealed from faith to faith" (Romans 1:16–17). Christ Himself seemed more inclined to use such language as "come," "learn," "eat," "drink," or "abide," but the thought seems to be the same: faith in Him was essential to having Him, and with Him salvation.

It is apparent that we have the same basic problem here that we had with repentance. The persons of whom it is required have no disposition toward it. If enemies of God will not repent of their enmity, certainly they are not

going to cultivate an affectionate trust in the God whom
they hate. Indeed Jesus said, "No man can come to me, except the Father which sent Me draw him" (John 6:44). He
warned the Pharisees that they did not come to Him "because you are not of My sheep" (John 10:26). "Except a
man be born again, he cannot see the kingdom of God . . .
he cannot enter the into the kingdom of God" (John 3:3,
5).

So, then, men are obliged to have a faith which they
simply do not have and which, if left to themselves, they
will not get. You cannot say "Try as they will, they cannot believe," for they will not even try, they have no desire to try. We cannot say that they are unable to believe,
but that they are unwilling to believe. If they were willing, they would be able. Nothing is stopping them—
nothing, that is, but their own unwillingness.

Their obligation is not in the slightest reduced because of their unwillingness. Why should it be? Since
when do a man's duties cease to exist simply because he is
unwilling to perform them? What would be left of the
moral law if men's unwillingness to obey it were sufficient
reason for abolishing it?

Granted that men are responsible for that which they
are indisposed to do, still the question remains of how
they are going to get the right disposition, especially
when they do not want it. If they wanted a right disposition, that would prove that they had one. Only a right
disposition seeks to be right. But since they do not have a
right disposition, we may assume that they have no inclination to get one either. They would be as indisposed toward getting a right disposition as toward any other obligation in God's law. So the problem is, how are persons
going to get a right disposition who do not want one?

This last observation needs to be qualified. Men do not, in one sense, want a new disposition, but there is another sense in which they do. They do not want it in the sense of loving it and desiring it for its own sake. But they do desire it because they know that if they do not have one they will suffer some very great pain and lose out on some very great pleasures. Now they do want to avoid pain and to have all possible pleasures, and in that sense they want what is necessary toward that end. They may not like the way to this goal, but they do like the goal; therefore, they choose the unwelcome way because of the welcome end. A boy may not like castor oil, but he does like to be outside playing; if castor oil is the only appointed way of getting outside, that fact may make him take it. He still does not like castor oil in and of himself, but he may "like" it as a means to an end which he does like.

Thus, when a man begins to seek a right disposition, he does so not because he likes it, but because he likes what goes with it. He still hates it, as the boy hates his castor oil, but he seeks it nonetheless. Please note that the man in question is not now accepting a right disposition (it has not yet been given to him), but he is concerned at this point about seeking to have it given to him.

Very well, the man with the wrong motive begins to seek for the right one. Driven by a fear of hell, he seeks for a love of heaven. Or, driven by a desire for the physical pleasure of heaven, he seeks for a disposition to love heaven for its own sake—for a disposition to yearn for that place where there is perfect fellowship with God and godly persons. What must he then do?

First, if he would have faith born in his soul he must acquaint himself with the Object of this faith. There is no

possibility of believing in someone who is unknown. If
the Christian gospel requires faith in Christ, then Christ
must be known. The man must read about Him as He is
presented in the Bible. He must ponder and meditate. All
this is quite within the power of his disposition. A man
can be a devil and still study the Bible and learn about
Jesus. It will probably be a dull business, because he has
no heart for such study, but that dullness will be overcome by the sense of urgency that drives him to this
study.

There are many misrepresentations of the nature of
Christ. Some think of Him as merely a human being;
some suppose that He was all sweetness and light, with no
sternness in His heart; some suppose that He was full of
promise but did not teach about the judgment of God and
the place where the fire is not quenched; some suppose
that He died because evil forces were too much for Him,
and that when He died this was simply an unhappy mistake; some even suppose that when He died that was the
end, except that His teaching and spirit survived the
tomb; some suppose that coming to Him and believing in
Him consist in nothing more than accepting some true
statements about Him.

The Jesus Christ of these suppositions has never
lived. He may be called Jesus, but the Jesus of history
bears nothing but the most superficial resemblance to
this caricature. This description is a figment of the imagination, and if anyone believes it that belief has no relation
to the true Christ. The Jesus thus described is someone
quite different, and there are no hopes offered to those
who believe in a different Jesus whom they have fabri-
cated out of the stuff that dreams are made of. The person
who is thinking of such a Christ is no nearer to the king-

dom than when he first began to reflect.

Rather, the first thing that the person who seeks the faith God has commanded of him must do is to think carefully, objectively, and without prejudice about Jesus Christ as He is actually presented in the biblical record. The Christ of the Bible is a true man, indeed, but also a man who could say that He and the Father were one (John 10:30), who was before Abraham (John 8:58), whose shoes the great Baptist was unworthy to unloose (John 1:27), who was coming again on clouds of glory to judge the nations (Mark 13:26), and who died and shed His blood for the remission of sin (Matthew 26:28). Without such essential knowledge of the Object of faith, faith itself is impossible.

Such knowledge, however, is by no means the same thing as faith in that Object of Whom we now have knowledge. To the unregenerate man, this Holy One of God is as repulsive as ever. The man is as far from faith as he ever was. He will never come to faith in a person whom he hates simply by studying about him, though he cannot come to faith in him without studying about him.

Learning about the Object of faith may be the first thing, but the next thing is to obey Him. It is one thing to know that Christ is the Son of God and the Savior of the world, and that He was a very holy being who commanded men to be holy; but there must also be an effort to become holy, at least insofar as it is possible without a good disposition. Of course, a person cannot be truly and fully holy without a good disposition. If he had an evil disposition and did some good things, all that would mean for him would be that "ye, then, being evil, know how to give good gifts" (Matthew 7:11). Still, it is true that he is able, without a good disposition, to give good gifts and do many good things—good when considered in themselves.

Thus such a man may avoid temptation, even though he loves it. He may cut off his hand and pluck out his eye, as it were, not because he loves the moral purity that Christ commanded, but because he wants to receive this gift that would bring what he does desire. So, without any love of purity, he would find himself avoiding the outward expression of adultery, or other situations that would expose him to temptation. He could not have a true love for God and the Lord's day without a new heart, but he could avoid working on the Sabbath and he could go to church on that day.

In short, it is within the power of a wicked disposition to contribute to the cause of God and His kingdom. The unregenerate man may not be able to circumcise his own heart so as to love his fellow man, but he can avoid murdering him or doing any other outward violence. As doing these right things is within the power of a depraved will, these acts would be necessary demonstrations that the person was seeking after a new heart. Failure to do these things would show indifference, and such a person could hope for nothing from God but judgment.

Now, if a person does all the above things, as he should do, he still has not placed God under the slightest obligation to him. He has done some good things, to be sure. He may have suffered considerably in the process. But he has done nothing out of love for God. Christ can still say to him, concerning all the devils he may have cast out in Christ's name, or all the prophecies he made in Christ's name, or all the wonderful works he has done, "I know you not . . . depart from Me, all ye workers of iniquity" (Luke 13:27). But apparently it is in the course of this seeking that God commonly bestows saving faith.

Such a gift from God is, in any case, a gift of grace. No man can merit it by anything. If God gives it, He does so without any obligation to do so. But when He does give it, it is common for Him to give it to those who agonize to enter the kingdom—to men who would strive to enter the kingdom of God by force, like soldiers determined to take a stronghold even if they die in the attempt (see Luke 13:24).

Now suppose that after a man has sought to understand Christ and to do all that was in his disposition to do in obedience to Christ, God does change his heart and give him a new disposition to love Christ and come to Him—that is, to believe in Him. Then what does this person do? He comes to Him, of course. But what does this coming mean? It means that he ceases to trust in himself for any supposed righteousness. He knows that he is a sinner, that there is no soundness in him, and that his "hope is built on nothing less than Jesus' blood and righteousness." He says, "Nothing in my hands I bring, simply to Thy cross I cling."

Before now, this man claimed righteousness for this or that reason; now he has none at all, except Christ. Before, he had this excuse or that alibi to offer for his misdemeanors, but now he has nothing to say about the ungodly deeds he has done, except to confess that they come from a yet more ungodly heart. He knows that justification is by faith alone, apart from the works of the law. He experiences the joy of the man to whom the Lord does not impute iniquity. Like the publican who went up to the temple to pray, he cannot so much as lift his eyes to heaven; he beats upon his breast and cries, "God be merciful to me a sinner" (Luke 18:13). And he goes "down to his house justified" (Luke 18:14) by faith in the mercy of God in Christ Jesus. In Paul's words, "Now to him that worketh not but believeth on him that justifieth the ungodly, his faith is counted to him for righteousness" (Romans 4:5).

This is saving faith, and this is all there really is to saving faith. But this faith expresses itself in good works. As John Calvin once wrote, "Justification is by faith alone, but not by the faith that is alone." That is to say, the faith that justifies is full of good works. Those works, however, are nothing other than this true faith in expression. They are not something separate from, detached from, or added on to faith; they are simply faith in action, faith in expression, faith in manifestation. As James writes, faith is "made perfect" in works (James 2:22); that is, faith reaches its goal (*telos*) or expression in works. So James rightly argues that faith without works is dead. What he means is that faith without works is not faith. Faith which does not express itself is not a living or true faith.

Notice how the classic statement of justification by faith alone (in Romans 4) and the classic statement of justification by works (in James 2) come to perfect agreement in the same man, Abraham, and the same Old Testament statement about him. Paul cites Abraham when he says that his faith was accounted to him as righteousness (Romans 4:3). Likewise, James cites the very same passage after he has referred to Abraham's willingness to sacrifice his son, Isaac, at the command of God. James does so to show that this good work of obedience was not the basis of his salvation, but rather it was evidence of his true faith, or an expression of it: "Abraham believed God, and it was imputed unto him for righteousness" (James 2:23).

So, then, the revealed duty of faith may be summarized. The unbeliever must learn to believe, although it is alien to an unbelieving heart. He does not have it in his unbelieving disposition to believe, but he does have it in his unbelieving heart to hate pain and love pleasure, and therefore to seek for the very faith which he does not love for the sake of those things he does love. He seeks this faith by learning about Christ, who is the Object of this faith, and by doing what is within the power of his unwilling disposition, such as outward conformity to the moral law as Christ commands. God still reserves the right to convert the man and give him faith or not as He chooses, since He is under no obligation to a man for doing good deeds from an evil motive. However, this doer may hope that God will have mercy on him and bestow a believing heart. If God does so, the person will recognize this gift by trusting in Christ altogether for his salvation and by letting this faith express itself inwardly and outwardly in accordance with the whole will of Christ.

This is not the common view of evangelism, but it is the true one. Ordinarily, modern evangelists assume that unconverted persons have a potential disposition to faith that can be activated by their preaching. However, persons "dead" in sin have no disposition or potential for faith. Faith comes by hearing—if it comes. Let sinners "seek" His gift of faith rather than try to produce it in utterly depraved hearts. That is the message of true evangelism.

Chapter 16

Church Membership and Discipline

The duties of the revealed moral law thus far citeded, repentance and faith, are internal duties. They pertain to the heart; although, if they are genuine, they will have outward expression. They themselves do not include that expression but are the principles from which it comes. Repentance and faith are the saving dispositions from which all saving expressions proceed. They are fundamental, but they are not alone. If they are alone they are not genuine, but spurious.

The essential and first expression of the new spirit is a love for the moral law. As we have said, that law belongs to all men, but not all men belong to it. It loves all men and would do all men good, but they are carnal and not subject to it. They will be condemned for not living by it, and they cannot be saved through its observance. Nevertheless, it is binding upon them; consequently, we presented it as relevant to all men, and as the point at which their concern for salvation usually comes to consciousness, although they are not saved by it. Conversion, which is the composite term for this faith and repentance of which we have spoken, produces in the heart a love for this law. "O how love I Thy law!" cries the Psalmist (Psalm 119:97). "The law is holy, just and true," says Paul (Romans 7:12). "After the inward man I serve the law" (Romans 7:22). This is the writing of the law on one's heart of which the prophets spoke, saying, "It is graven upon the table of their heart, and upon the horns of your altars" (Jeremiah 17:1).

So the moral law is not different for the converted person than for the unconverted person, but the person himself is different. The law has not changed, but the lawkeeper has. He now keeps the law not only externally, as he may have done when unconverted, but from deep affection for it. He recognizes the law as an expression of the nature of a holy God, Whom he now loves since he has a new heart made after God's image. Because he loves the law, he meditates on it day and night (Psalm 1:2). Thus he comes to understand it far better than he previously did when he considered it only because he felt forced to do so, and when he was prone to consider it only as far as it fell within his power to keep it, namely, in its superficial and external meaning.

But since the law is no different for the Christian than for the non-Christian, and since we have already considered it in its general application, we need not review it again here. We have said all that needs to be said about what does become different after conversion. We may, therefore, go on to consider new duties that arise from the conversion experience. These are duties that belong peculiarly to the Christian (although, as we have already noted, there is a sense in which they pertain to unbelievers as well, indirectly, inasmuch as unbelievers should be believers and thus should keep these duties too). Since their direct application is only to Christians, and since these duties come to us by special rather than natural revelation, we take them up at this point.

Very well, then, assuming that we have a new principle of life in Christ Jesus, what expression of this principle is required? In using the term "required" we do not mean to suggest that the duties we are about to discuss are imposed from without, and contrary to the person on whom they are imposed, rather than spontaneous. We say "required" because, although the new heart is disposed to do all that the Lord its God commands, it still needs to be told what those commands are. It no doubt has a natural impulse, after this supernatural change, to have fellowship with others who have enjoyed the same transformation. No doubt, if there were no command from heaven not to forsake the assembling of believers together (Hebrews 10:25), Christians would have assembled anyway, by natural impulse. At the same time, there may have been some misgiving about doing so if it were not specifically commanded. Furthermore, the remaining corruption of the saints would have inclined them to laziness in this activity. So a command was necessary, and it was given.

An unfortunate habit of failing to attend church, except at irregular intervals, has developed in our time. Some have even said that it is a Roman Catholic notion that church attendance is necessary, while the Protestant comes to church when and if he desires to do so. It is true that the Roman church requires attendance, but it is false that the Protestant church does not. *Both* churches require attendance; the difference between them is the reason given for attending. The Romanist comes because his church (which he thinks has the authority of God) requires it; the Protestant comes because the Bible (which he thinks is the Word of God) requires it.

Let us be very clear on this. The traditional Protestant church teaches that it is a violation of the express requirements of Scripture for any Christian to be absent from church unless physically unable to attend. The delinquent church attender is living in sin. Absenteeism is immorality. God will not hold him guiltless who takes His name in vain (by professing it without worshiping Him).

Joining the church is the first, but not the last step to churchmanship. Granted that there is an obligation to join and to attend, it goes without saying that one should attend in the right spirit. That is, there should be reverence in the house of God, careful attentiveness to the means of grace and to the exposition of Scripture, and the like.

It is a duty incumbent on church members to support their denomination financially. If it is evident from natural ethics that every man owes all he possesses to God, it will be immediately apparent that once a person has become a Christian, he owes it to God to express the stewardship of his means by giving to the church which God has established and commanded him to join and attend.

A man may object here, "I can see how I may owe my salvation to God and should thank Him for that and perhaps show my gratitude for it by tithing or by giving in some proportionate measure. Still, I do not see how this is a duty. It may be an impulse, but why a duty? After all, I did not earn my salvation but I do earn my daily bread. Why do I owe any of that to anyone, even God? I agree with Charles Lamb who once expressed the sentiment that he felt more like offering grace before a good book than before a meal, for he thought he had earned the meal but not the book. Have I not earned my own money if not my salvation?"

Have you really? If God had not given you birth,

would you have been able to earn your bread? If God had not given you health and preserved you to this very moment, could you have earned it? Can you take credit for having been born where you were, in a land where you could find employment?

But most of all, you should be grateful to God not only that you can earn your daily bread, but that you are made in such a way that earning your bread is itself a delightful act. Men sometimes think that they work only in order to live, but as soon as they are stricken with paralysis or some other confining impediment, they would give anything to be able to work again. Even if their insurance is paying all their expenses, and even if they have sufficient money to live comfortably, they still wish they could work. Under such circumstances it becomes evident that men owe even more gratitude to God for the ability and inclination to work, perhaps, than simply for the bread they thereby earn.

The above considerations, then, contrary to excusing a person from the duty of giving to God and His church, provide an additional reason for doing so.

Not only are attending and contributing financially to the church part of a member's duty, but so is helping in any other way such as teaching. We hardly need to develop the observation that a Christian should do all he possibly can for the glory of God. A man who has the opportunity to serve God and does not take it cannot possibly be a Christian, for such behavior would mean that he is not truly grateful for what God has done. And if he is not grateful for the infinite gift of eternal salvation, how could he conceivably believe in it?

A further obligation with respect to the church is that, in addition to walking in a fashion worthy of one's calling, one should see to it, insofar as possible, that others who profess the same faith walk in the same way. The church is a covenanting society; that is, members bind themselves together to watch over each other's souls as well as their own. This discipline rests formally in the hands of the church officers, especially the ministers, but to a lesser extent it belongs to all believers.

As a corollary to this obligation, all believers must sympathize with this difficult work of discipline, even though sanctions may be brought against oneself or one's family. The purity of God's house, and its integrity before the world to which it witnesses, must take priority over the feelings of any of its members. The implementation of discipline will be less difficult if all members understand the need for it and cooperate in its administration.

Some suppose that discipline, because it involves judging, is contrary to the law of Christ, and for this reason they have misgivings about it. They cite His words, "Judge not, that ye be not judged" (Matthew 7:1), as justification for permitting a person to live in adultery, or with an unconfessed bank embezzlement, or as a dishonest judge or corrupt public official, without taking any steps to bring this person to repentance or remove him from the church. We need not go into an exposition of Christ's words here, except to say that they cannot possibly mean what this objection would suppose. If they did mean that no Christian should ever administer discipline, they would make Christ, who commanded in Matthew 18 that they do just that, look quite foolish.

We may further make the general observation that what the Christian religion forbids, when it speaks against judging, is censoriousness. That is, we are not to condemn other persons while presuming that we ourselves are without fault, nor are we to condemn the motives of another, since the person exercising judgment cannot possibly know these. In discipline, there is no place for a censorious spirit. In fact, the officers of the church are told to act in a "spirit of meekness" (Galatians 6:1), that is, to realize that they themselves have the same tendency toward corruption in their hearts, and that nothing but the grace of God has preserved them from its expression.

When church discipline is carried out, the persons administering it do not act in their own name. On the contrary, they act in Christ's name and by His appointment. Recognizing their own weakness and frailty, they proceed in a penitent spirit, motivated only by obedience to God's command and by zeal that the church of God should be kept pure of all gross violations of God's law.

So, then, there is a certain humility involved in administering discipline, if it is done properly. The persons administering it do so in obedience and humble subservience to Christ. They do not do their own will, which would most often favor the far simpler and lazier course of ignoring the evil deeds and avoiding the painful steps involved in correcting it. They do not assert their own will, but the will of Christ. This is not arrogance, but meekness and submissiveness. On the other hand, the person who refuses to carry out discipline when Christ has commanded that it be done is exceedingly arrogant. He has the audacity to disobey God, to assert his own will and wisdom above God's commands. This is consummate pride. Furthermore, to make matters worse, he claims the motive for his evil deed is humility. He says that he does not feel superior to other persons, and that therefore he will not discipline them. In so speaking, he feels and acts superior to God whose commands he disregards. This is adding gall to disobedience.

The church member should understand the nature of discipline and not only keep himself from becoming liable to it, but help to keep others from it, and also cooperate with the authorities in administering it when it is necessary and desirable.

So, then, the ideal for a Christian is to be a good member of the church, the body of Christ, and to help others to be the same, in order that the world may know that those inside the church have truly been touched by Christ.

Chapter 17

Use of the Means of Grace: The Word of God

In the preceding chapter we considered the converted person's obligation to unite with the church of Jesus Christ and to submit himself to all due authority in that church. These authorities, whether ministers or other officers, have the care of souls as those who must give account, and therefore the people are to seek wisdom at the priest's mouth, as it was phrased in the Old Testament.

The ministry is especially charged with the study and teaching of the Word of God. Scripture places a premium on the minister's responsibility to bear witness to the light of truth. Not only is the minister called a lamp, but the Word of God is also called a lamp for our feet (Psalm 119:105). It is appropriate that the minister and the Word should be thus identified. For what is the minister's message but the Word, and who is the Word's voice but the minister? "Teach the children of Israel all the statutes which the Lord hath spoken" (Leviticus 10:11).

To the reluctant and fearful Jeremiah, God said, "Say not, I am a child: for thou shalt go to all that I shall send thee, and whatsoever I command thee thou shalt speak. . . . Gird up thy loins, and arise, and speak unto them all that I command thee: be not dismayed at their faces, lest I confound thee before them" (Jeremiah 1:7, 17). "The prophet that hath a dream, let him tell a dream; and

he that hath My word, let him speak My word faithfully"
(Jeremiah 23:28). "I will give you pastors according to
Mine heart, which shall feed you with knowledge and understanding" (Jeremiah 3:15). "For the priest's lips shall
keep knowledge," said Malachi, "and they shall seek the
law at his mouth: for he is the messenger of the Lord of
hosts" (Malachi 2:7).

Just before His ascension Christ commanded all His
disciples to go into all the world making disciples of all
nations and "teaching them to observe all things whatsoever I have commanded you" (Matthew 28:19–20). And
Paul said that "the servant of the Lord must not strive;
but be gentle unto all men, apt to teach, patient, in meekness instructing those that oppose themselves; if God
peradventure will give them repentance to the acknowledging of the truth; and that they may recover themselves out of the snare of the devil, who are taken captive
by him at his will" (2 Timothy 2:24–26).

While the minister is an authoritative, divinely appointed expositor of the Word of God for the edification of
the people, the people themselves have direct access to
the Bible. They, of course, cannot devote their full time to
its study. Their secular earnings go toward the support of
those who are official ministers, so that these men may
devote themselves fully to the ministry of the Word, and
thus they "communicate unto him that teacheth in all
good things" (Galatians 6:6).

At the same time, the ministers are to instruct the
people in such a way that the people may learn to study
for themselves. It is sometimes said of teachers that their
job is to teach their pupils to become no longer dependent on the teacher. This is not quite the function of a
minister toward his congregation, as he is to teach them

to become only partly independent of him. He remains always the only official interpreter and expositor, and the people retain some need for his help. But they are also to study for themselves, and they too have "an unction from the Holy One" so that the ministers are not alone responsible to "know all things" (1 John 2:20).

Two extremes must be avoided in this matter. The first is the notion that only ordained persons may interpret and understand the Word of God, and the other is that the people can not only interpret the Word of God, but interpret it as well and as authoritatively as the minister himself. There is no difference in kind between clergy and laity, but there is a difference of degree. What God has joined together (in that both ministers and lay persons may interpret Scripture), let not man put asunder; but what God has differentiated, in establishing a relation of superior and inferior, let not man equate.

Both minister and people have a duty to study the Word of God. The minister does not have more obligation to study it than his people, but he has an obligation to study it more than his people. It is incumbent on godly persons, be they ministers or not, to meditate on the Bible and lay up its truths in their hearts.

The people must study the Word of God, for there is no possible life in Christ apart from it. We have already noted that, even before conversion, a person is obliged to study the Bible, especially as it pertains to Christ and to believing in Him. If this is important before conversion, how much more so afterwards. If it is important in order to be reborn, it is even more essential to maintaining the life that is born.

We may state this duty in a formula as follows: a person may understand sound biblical doctrine without be-

ing saved, but he cannot be saved without understanding
sound biblical doctrine. A person may have a supply of
food yet die of starvation, but if a person is to stay alive
he must have a supply of food. It would be exceedingly
strange, in the physical realm, for anyone to have food
available yet die of starvation; but in the spiritual realm it
is far from uncommon. Many have a knowledge of the
biblical message who do not accept it, for one reason or
another, and therefore, in the midst of spiritual plenty,
they die.

There are many instances of those who know the
Bible's truths but perish nonetheless. For example,
Christ condemned the Pharisees, in general, for although
they were close students of the law they strained at the
gnat and swallowed the camel (Matthew 23:24). Although
they knew the way into the kingdom of heaven, they
would not enter themselves, nor permit others to go in.
Hence, in spite of their knowledge, they were not saved.

Christ performed only one miracle of cursing. He
cursed the fig tree because it had leaves, which gave an
indication of fruit, yet had no fruit (Matthew 21:19). He
was not, of course, angry with the tree, but was using it
to warn those who, like the tree, made a profession on
which they did not follow through. They knew the truth
and even professed to accept it, but their inward rejection
was made evident by their lack of fruit.

Paul, similarly, says of the heathen world before
Christ that it held "the truth in unrighteousness"
(Romans 1:18). That is to say, they too knew something of
the revelation of God in nature, conscience, and history,
but even though knowing God they did not worship Him
as God. They had knowledge without life. In 2 Timothy
3:7 there is a description of some persons who were "ever

learning and never able to come to the knowledge of the truth." So it is possible for persons to know much of the content of God's revelation without coming to it, accepting it, or living by it. Another Bible writer warns against being hearers but not doers of the Word (James 1:22), again showing that it is possible to hear and understand the Word of God without receiving it and translating it into life.

Not only it is possible for men to know Bible truth without being saved, but in this case it will prove to have been better for them had they never known it. He who has much light, yet does not live according to that light, "shall be beaten with many stripes" (Luke 12:47). "To whom much is given, of him shall much be required" (see Luke 12:48) is a doctrine of both special and natural revelation. It is obvious to all persons that the more we have, the more we will be responsible for. We cannot be responsible for anything unless we have it; but, by the same token, the more of it we have, for that much more shall we be held accountable. It will be more tolerable for Sodom than for Capernaum in the day of judgment, not because Capernaum was naturally more wicked than Sodom, but because she had greater light and opportunity for salvation than Sodom. Publicans and harlots are nearer to the kingdom than scribes and Pharisees, in the sense that, if hell were opened and the captives loosed, those who were least guilty would be released first. Though all of these are sinners, the religious sinners have more light than the nonreligious sinners.

The danger facing those who hear but do not obey the Word is a most sobering aspect of this duty to learn the truth. But the other side of the formula must also be remembered—namely, that we cannot be saved without holding the truth. In 2 Thessalonians 2:13 we read that "God hath from the beginning chosen you to salvation through sanctification of the Spirit and belief of the truth." In other words, those whom God has chosen for salvation, He brings to it by means of belief in the truth. Occasionally someone asks why, if predestination is true, it makes any difference whether he does anything to come to God or not. "If I am predestined for salvation," goes the objection, "I will be saved, no matter what." But such is not the case, as this text shows.

In Romans 10 Paul dwells at length on the tremendous importance of hearing and coming to believe in the Word of God. "How shall they believe in him of whom they have not heard? and how shall they hear without a preacher? . . . Faith cometh by hearing, and hearing by the Word of God" (Romans 10:14–17). This tells us in very clear terms that no one can be saved without hearing the Word of truth, and therefore it is imperative to have missionaries who will convey that essential gospel.

Christ, in His farewell prayer recorded in John 17, prays that God would sanctify His beloved disciples by His truth. "Thy Word," He continues, "is truth." Thus the way by which the followers of Christ are to be made Christlike, or sanctified, is by the knowledge of the Word of God. This is the sword of the Spirit. He uses it to remove the remaining corruptions of the heart and to induce new graces and glory in the Christian soul. It cannot be done any other way. And no other way is necessary, since this one is available.

The *Westminster Shorter Catechism* summarizes this matter excellently when it says, "The Spirit of God maketh the reading, but especially the preaching, of the Word an effectual means of convincing and converting sinners, and building them up in holiness and comfort through faith unto salvation." In the same context the catechism tells us that if the Word is to be effectual to salvation we must "attend thereunto with diligence, preparation, and prayer, receive it with faith and love, lay it up in our hearts, and practice it in our lives."

Practicing it in our lives is an important part of studying and understanding the Word of God. In this sense it is not altogether different from other books. All subjects are better understood if they are practiced—if there is laboratory work to go along with the textbook. The principles are understood better and more accurately when they are applied in practice or experiment. If this is advisable for all studies, it is absolutely essential for Bible study. "If any man will do His will, he shall know of the doctrine," said Christ (John 7:17). There is, therefore, no saving knowledge, apparently—no ultimately meaningful knowledge of the Word of God—apart from doing the will of God.

Why is it that the practice of the Word is absolutely essential to its understanding? For this reason: if the Word of God says something and the person does not practice it, that creates a hopeless tension. If one man received teaching from another man and then did not follow it, that would not necessarily create a problem, for one man is not, in the last analysis, the servant of another. Man is, however, the servant of God, and a servant is not greater than his Lord. When a man says "No" to God, he creates an impossible situation; he cannot do that and live with his conscience or his mind. He simply cannot do it unless he has become a devil. He must obey, or else he must twist the commandment. There is no other alternative.

Let us assume that a man who calls himself a creature of God is unwilling to do what the Bible teaches him. What will he then do? As we have just said, he cannot flatly refuse to obey. He must wrest the Scripture. He must interpret the commandment to teach other than it does. He must bring his obligations in line with his lusts. The Word of God must bend to the will of the creature.

The situation is not unlike the experience of a man who had a picture of the leaning tower of Pisa hanging on his wall. Each morning, when he came to his office, he found the picture hanging askew. Finally he inquired of the maid how it happened that each morning when he came in he found the picture hanging crooked. She explained that she had to turn it that way in order to make the tower hang straight. In the same fashion, men whose lives are crooked and who will not make them upright have no alternative but to turn the teaching of the Word of God so that is squares with their practices.

What this does to the interpretation of the Bible is painfully clear. It means that the wicked simply will not let the Word of God have free course in their lives. They will be unable to interpret it correctly, for they refuse ever to understand anything in the Bible which cuts across the grain of their own inclinations. On the other hand, if they are ever going to divide rightly the Word of truth, they must repent and conform their lives to its teachings. They must have the disposition of Samuel who said, "Speak, Lord; for Thy servant heareth" (1 Samuel 3:9). Of Christ it was written, "In the volume of the book it is written of me, I delight to do Thy will, O my God: yes, Thy law is within my heart" (Psalm 40:7). "If therefore thine eye be single, thy whole body shall be full of light" (Matthew 6:22). The pure in heart shall see God (Matthew

5:8) and the Word of God.

So once again we find ourselves within the virtuous circle. The Word of God is a means of grace; that is, it tends to produce grace in the soul. It is the means by which the disciples of Christ are saved and sanctified. At the same time that the Word is necessary for gracious living, however, gracious living also is necessary in order to understand the Word of God. If we do not have the Word in our souls we will not live graciously, and if we do not live graciously we will not understand the Word. But conversely, if we do have the Word of God in our souls we shall have a tendency to live graciously, and as we live graciously we shall have more and more of the Word in our souls.

Chapter 18

Use of the Means of Grace: Prayer

We will consider prayer as a means of grace between the chapters on the Word and the Spirit, because prayer comes between the Word and the Spirit. It is the principal means by which one secures the Spirit's guidance to enable the reader to understand the Word and be sanctified thereby. Prayer itself has no efficacy except as it lays hold of the power of God, and the power of God is the Spirit of God.

This fact brings prayer into a close relation to duty. It is not only a duty itself, but also a power that makes it possible to carry out other duties. If the Spirit is the source of power by which morals rise up and walk, as we shall see in the next chapter—that is, the power by which we carry out our moral duty—prayer is the key to this power, and so indirectly it is the power. Therefore, prayer is a moral obligation underlying all moral obligation; we are obliged to pray because we are obliged to all duty. Prayer is not only a part of that duty, but a means to fulfill the remainder of it.

It may be helpful at this point to compare and contrast the prayer of unregenerate nature and the prayer of regenerate nature. The natural man's prayer emerges from his misery, selfishness, and sinfulness. God is not pleased with it. In fact, it is obnoxious to Him, even though He sometimes hears and answers, out of sheer mercy upon their wretchedness, sinful men whose prayers are an abomination to Him. In the case of His own children the matter is quite different. They too have sin, and their prayers contain sin, which is obnoxious to God. But they are in Christ Jesus Who ever lives to make intercession for them; He prays for them even as they pray. Because Christ is pleasing in God's sight, His prayer on their behalf is heard, and thus their prayer is heard. (This, incidentally, indicates the reason why all availing prayer must necessarily be in the name and Spirit of Christ.) Furthermore, by their regeneration the believers have a nature which partakes of the spirit of the divine nature (1 Peter 1:4) and is therefore partially pleasing to God in its own right. Its remaining sinfulness would utterly disqualify it, however, were it not for the continuing intercession of Christ who interposes the benefits of His precious blood.

John Chrysostom, the golden-mouthed preacher of the fifth century, explained the nature of Christ's intercession in the life of prayer with this story. There was in Constantinople a boy who loved his father very greatly. Since the father was about to return home after a long absence, his son prepared a gift for him. Knowing how much his father loved flowers, the boy gathered a bouquet and showed it to his mother as the gift he would present on his father's return. The mother saw a bouquet indeed—one made up of weeds as well as flowers, a hopeless assortment of colors, the stems of varying lengths. Appreciating the child's intentions, she took the bouquet, removed the weeds, trimmed the stems, and arranged the flowers in a colorful ensemble. This became the bouquet which the boy presented to his father. Likewise Christ takes our misshapen utterances which we call prayers and, by His grace, removes its offensive aspects and presents a thing of beauty and efficacy to the Father, in Christ's own name.

Let us now consider the structure of prayer as a guide to the fulfillment of this Christian duty. The Lord Himself was pleased to give us a pattern prayer to guide all subsequent ages as they come to the throne of grace in times of need. Although the Lord's Prayer is known to all Christians, we shall repeat it here for clarity of reference to its petitions: "Our Father Which art in heaven, Hallowed be Thy name. Thy kingdom come. Thy will be done in earth, as it is in heaven. Give us this day our daily bread. And forgive us our debts, as we forgive our debtors. And lead us not into temptation, but deliver us from evil" (Matthew 6:9–13). The doxology commonly added in the recitation of this prayer was probably a later addition to the words of Christ and need not be considered here.

The preface to the prayer, "Our Father Which art in heaven," teaches two contrasting aspects of the approach to God in prayer. He is to be addressed as "our Father," not "my Father," and, at the same time, we are to remember that He is a Father Who is in heaven. This combines the utmost in intimacy and respect within the same salutation. When we are permitted to address the eternal God as Father, we are permitted the greatest familiarity of access to Him in Whose presence the angels cover their faces. Lest, however, there should be any foolish presuming upon such a superlative privilege, we are immediately told to address him as the Father Who is in heaven, thus reminding us that as near as God may be to us in His Fatherhood, He is, at the same time, infinitely removed from us, as far as heaven is from earth and indeed infinitely further. Familiarity, so far from being permitted to breed contempt, is combined with a sense of the great transcendence of the exalted God Who is infinitely above His creatures and Whom, indeed, the heaven of heavens cannot contain.

The first petition is "Hallowed be Thy name." It is in this petition, as we have observed before, that we avoid violating the third commandment, "Thou shalt not take the name of the Lord thy God in vain." His name is His person and His attributes, and all His deeds by which these are manifested. Fully conscious of the greatness and holiness of God, the prayer that comes from the heart would sanctify that glorious and exalted Being and would desire that all things be disposed according to His purpose, so as to reveal His glory in the earth and everywhere else.

The second petition requests the coming of God's kingdom. *The Shorter Catechism* gives an excellent explanation of the full meaning of this petition. It states that with these words we ask that "Satan's kingdom may be destroyed, and that the kingdom of grace may be advanced, ourselves and others brought into it, and kept in it, and that the kingdom of glory may be hastened."

The kingdom of God is the area in which God reigns as King over subjects (in the next petition, we will see what kind of subjects; for now, there is simply the request that God might reign). But, if God is to reign, his great adversary's reign must be destroyed. Satan, the sworn enemy of all that is holy, who attempts to frustrate the advance of God's glory—especially in the souls of men—must be stopped and crushed. But this happens only as men are delivered from the power of him who holds them captive to his will (2 Timothy 2:26) and who rules as the prince of the power of the air, the spirit that now works in the children of disobedience (Ephesians 2:2). Thus, in this petition we are praying that God will translate men out of the kingdom of darkness and into the kingdom of His dear Son (Colossians 1:13).

But it is not enough that we be brought into that kingdom, for Satan will continue to pursue us. Since he is far too strong for us and could easily take us again in his snare, by this petition we ask that we be kept safe by God's power unto eternal salvation (1 Peter 1:5). This is our hope for the everlasting kingdom from which all that offends God has been removed and which is the perfect realization of the reign of God over men. This is the kingdom of glory for which the saints of God are always eagerly waiting. Because of this hope they purify themselves as He is pure in whom they hope. Thus this second petition begins by calling for the destruction of Satan's kingdom and ends with the consummation of the kingdom of God in heaven.

The third petition is "Thy will be done in earth as it is in heaven." This is not merely a request that God's will be done, but that it be done in a particular manner. The sincere Christian is aware that God makes even the wrath of men to praise Him, that He rules over the unruly, and that there is nothing that ever comes to pass unless the Lord has commanded it (Lamentations 3:37). But he especially desires that he and all men do the will of God *intentionally*, with genuine affection for God rather than hatred, voluntarily rather than accidentally, spontaneously rather than by force. In short, he desires that people show the kind of obedience that is displayed by the angels in heaven, not the kind shown by devils in hell or sinners on earth—although, in an ultimate sense, all, whether willingly or unwillingly, do the will of the sovereign God.

The fourth petition is "Give us this day our daily bread." Here we begin the second part of the prayer, the part dealing specifically with our own human needs in distinction from the glory of God. Of course, glorifying God is the greatest of human needs; but here we are referring to our immediate, obvious needs. It is noteworthy that we do not pray for such needs until we have concerned ourselves with the glory, kingdom, and will of God. We do not even ask for our daily bread, as important as we may think that to be, until we have first asked that God's will be done.

But now, as we come to this second group of petitions, we are surprised to find at the top of the list not our spiritual but our temporal needs. Before we ask for the forgiveness of sins, we are taught to ask for our daily bread. Why is this? Does it mean our physical existence is more important than our spiritual needs? Hardly. But it shows the practicality of the Bible, and of the Lord, in acknowledging that our physical needs do take precedence over our spiritual ones in one sense: the precedence of necessity. We cannot have our sins forgiven unless we are alive to ask forgiveness. We must exist in order to receive forgiveness or any other spiritual gift.

The fifth petition is "Forgive us our debts as we forgive our debtors." This petition raises the ethical question in its sharpest focus, for it deals with the remission of ethical offenses. "Debts" are sins of omission which inevitably involve sins of commission as well. If I fail to show my parents respect, I thereby show them disrespect. In this petition we ask that these sins might be forgiven. But if they may be forgiven, does that mean they may freely be committed? That is, do we have any incentive to moral living if God Himself will forgive immoral living? Many ethicists suppose, because of this problem, that forgiveness is incompatible with morality.

But is this so? The petition does not assume that debts will be forgiven. After all, this is a prayer, or a request. If it is a prayer, then forgiveness is not automatic. To be sure, Christ teaches men to offer this prayer, and if He did not intend to encourage them to believe their sins could be forgiven He would not have told them to ask. But the petition itself also asserts a condition: "as we forgive our debtors."

If morality seems to be excluded by the first part of the petition, it just as evidently is asserted in the latter part. When we request forgiveness of our debts *as we have forgiven others*, we are asking conditionally. Furthermore, the condition is an ethical one: "forgive us if we have forgiven others." In other words, the very petition presumes a moral attitude. Only those who are of a forgiving and loving disposition may make this prayer fruitfully. Christ in the parable of the debtors (Matthew 18:23–34) shows the utter futility of making this prayer if one does not have such a disposition.

While this petition shows the place of moral law, it is not legalistic. It does not teach that we may be forgiven *because* we have forgiven others. That would be an absurd petition because it would make forgiveness, which is by definition undeserved, something we have earned by doing the good deed of forgiving others. If the petition were based on our own merit in forgiving others, it would give God no option but to grant us the forgiveness we deserve. God would be indebted to us, not we to Him. No, the spirit of the prayer is that inasmuch as we have the spirit of forgiveness, this is some indication of our sincerity in making our request of God, and therefore we may be encouraged in our asking.

"And lead us not into temptation, but deliver us from evil." Like the preceding petition, this one too seems inimical to fundamental moral principles. It would cause some to wonder about the propriety of introducing the Lord's Prayer in a book on ethics. Temptation, they would say, is necessary to moral trial, and a person must achieve deliverance from evil himself if he is going to show himself to be moral.

But is it an immoral impulse to fear temptation? Only if there is nothing to fear. But is there really nothing to fear? Are we sure that we are immutably good and therefore cannot be tempted and fall? God could not voice this petition, for He cannot be tempted and cannot sin. But what man is there who possesses such inalienable virtue? And if we do not, should we walk with an ethical chip on our shoulders? Should we be inviting temptation? Should we not rather pray not to be led into it? Is that prayer not both rational and ethical?

The second part of this petition indicates that the first part may not be granted. We would not be taught to ask God to deliver us from evil if we knew He would never expose us to temptation. Knowing that God may have some benign purpose in permitting us to face temptation, we pray that He will keep us from succumbing to it. Having acknowledged our weakness in the first part ("lead us not into temptation"), we now call upon God's strength in the second part ("and deliver us from evil"). We know that if God sees fit to subject us to temptation He means it for our good. Since the only way in which good can come out of temptation is by our conquering it, we ask God to give us conquering strength.

Is it immoral to ask for God's help in moral living? If we asked God to do what we are called on to do, that would be immoral. But what is wrong with asking God to keep us from sinning? As a matter of fact, is there any other way to keep from sinning than by God's help? And if this is so, is not our duty, rather than the abandonment of duty, to call upon God for help in time of need? On the other hand, does not pride go before a fall?

Just as we must have a forgiving disposition if we would hope that God will forgive us, so we must be opposed to evil if we expect God to deliver us from it. Thus the same Christ who teaches us to pray, "Lead us not into temptation," also teaches us to "Watch and pray, that ye enter not into temptation" (Matthew 26:41), and to cut off our hand or pluck out our eye rather than unnecessarily expose us to sin (Matthew 5:29–30). After all, we are neither identical with God (as in pantheism) and thereby free from danger, nor completely detached from God (as in deism) and unable to call on Him for help. Man, though separate from God, was made for union with God. This dependence on Him is at once the end and the means of ethical living.

Chapter 19

Use of the Means of Grace:
The Holy Spirit

In the Sermon on the Mount, Christ, after having described the exacting nature of the moral law turns to the topic of prayer. No doubt He intends that we should not be dismayed by the demands of Christian morality, and therefore He gives us a means by which we may lay hold of the power of God, which is completely sufficient for our moral needs. Indeed, in that entire sermon the commands are so stringent as to be discouraging, and the only bright spot of hopeful assurance is that prayer is available as a means to secure God's power. We remember again Augustine's famous words, "Give what You command and command what You will." This is prayer's response to the high demands of holiness. God cannot command too much as long as we are able to address ourselves to Him and secure His strength by which to accomplish His assignments.

No doubt it is part of God's purpose, in laying such impossible commands upon His servants, that they should repair to Him for aid. Were they able to do His will without His strength, they could also live without Him. But God has graciously ordained that we cannot do His will without His power, thereby making it impossible to live without Him. Thus the Psalmist writes that to live apart from God is death. If men would live, they must live in God. But what could be more wonderful than to live in God? This is more glorious than life itself. God through His severity is only pursuing a kindly policy to ensure our life with Him forever.

But just how does prayer bring God and His power to us? How does it become the dynamic of ethics? It is not because it has efficacy in itself. Rather, it is the means by which we secure the power of the Spirit to understand and apply the efficacy of the Word. But while prayer secures the power of the Spirit, it is the Spirit who inclines us to pray in the first place. This is what we called the virtuous circle.

Furthermore, the Spirit is not only the bond uniting the believer to the written Word, but also to the incarnate Word, Jesus Christ Himself. The Spirit is often called the Spirit of Christ, and He is the person of the Godhead by means of whom there is union with all the members of the Godhead. The Spirit takes the things of Christ and declares them unto us. Only he who has the Spirit of Christ belongs to Christ. If the Father is the person of the Godhead who *decrees* redemption, and the Son is the one who *procures* redemption, the Spirit is the one who *applies* it.

If, on the one hand, it is the Spirit who applies Christ and all His benefits to the believer, on the other hand the sum of all Christ's benefits has been purchased for us by the Spirit. Thus, when Christ teaches believers to pray confidently and insistently, he indicates that the primary gift they should pray for is the Spirit. "If ye then, being evil, know how to give good gifts unto your children: how much more shall your heavenly Father give the Holy Spirit to them that ask him?" (Luke 11:13).

Christ has purchased many things for us by His redemption, but do they not, in the last analysis, reduce to the purchase of God Himself? That is, can we not say that the Mediator's act of reconciling believers to God is ultimately the only aim of His work? To be sure, he secured remission of sin, adoption into the family of God, righteousness, wisdom, sanctification, and glorification. But all these are but parts of man's reunion with the God from Whom sin had estranged him. Even the temporal blessings of this life, which are also part of the purchase bought by Christ, are but means of keeping us alive so that we could enjoy that for which we live, namely God. There are rewards for those who, patiently continuing in good deeds, await glory, honor, and immortality; but these rewards consist essentially in a greater capacity to experience the infinite God. For what does a Christian work toward, when he aims at a more abundant entrance into glory, but to see Christ and God more clearly? The person by whom all this happens—by whom the Godhead resides in the believer's soul—is the third person of the Trinity, the Spirit. It is He Whom Christ came to purchase for His own, and it is He in Whom the saints' redemption truly consists.

This same Spirit Who is the bond of union between God and believers is also the bond of union between true believers. He is the basis of the communion of the saints; in a sense He is the communion of the saints. For it is by their common possession of the Spirit that believers are one in each other. Theirs is a vital union because this life principle of God is theirs also. Though only in a finite measure, because they are finite beings, they have the same type of union which obtains in the Godhead, namely, a union in the essence of the Godhead. This is what the Lord seems to have prayed for in John 17:21–23:

"That they all may be one; as Thou, Father, art in Me, and I in Thee, that they also may be one in Us: that the world may believe that Thou hast sent Me. And the glory which Thou gavest Me I have given them; that they may be one, even as We are one: I in them, and Thou in Me, that they may be made perfect in one; and that the world may know that Thou hast sent Me, and hast loved them, as Thou hast loved Me."

This, incidentally, reveals the difference between the brotherhood of believers and the brotherhood of man in general. All men have a common brotherhood in creation; but believers also have a brotherhood in redemption. All men have a brotherhood by participating in the same human nature; believers also have a unique participation in the divine nature. While Christians, therefore, experience the unity that all men have, they have in addition a union which other men do not have and which is infinitely more glorious. To obliterate the distinction between the two types of brotherhood does great violence to the Word of God and to the experience of true Christians.

If we have a Christian duty to seek the Spirit, let us see now how the Spirit enables us to do our duty. We may consider, for guidance in this discussion, Philippians 2:12–13: "Work out your own salvation with fear and trembling, for God is working in you to will and to do according to His good pleasure." We have already observed that the person of the Godhead who applies redemption and, therefore, may be said to be "working in [us] to will and to do" is the third person, the Holy Spirit. So this passage teaches us that the Spirit is at work in Christians.

How is the Spirit at work? Note first, negatively, that He is not at work in them to will and to do what they are supposed, as moral beings, to will and do. He works in them so that *they* may will and do. The Spirit does not do the willing and the doing; that is still men's prerogative. Men's willing and doing cannot, by definition, be done by anyone but men; if the Spirit were doing it, it would no longer be men's willing. And in that case we would have a pantheism which would obliterate the distinctiveness of the human individual and dissolve all in God. Men might still appear to be doing these things, but actually the invisible Spirit would be doing them; hence there would be no human personality left, nor any freedom or virtue, nor anything but God. So, then, we can say that however the Spirit works, He does not work in such a way that man ceases to work.

Second, again speaking negatively, although the Spirit's work does not obliterate the reality of human working, neither, on the other hand, does the reality of human working obliterate the role of the Spirit. In other words, if sanctification is not all of God, neither is it all of men. The passage in Philippians indicates that God is working "in you to will and to do." So, although the willing and the doing are truly of men, they are not solely of men, but God is involved somehow in the virtuous actions. If it is pantheistic and not Christian to suppose that God and not man is involved in producing virtue, it is humanistic and not Christian to suppose that man is working and not God.

The Spirit, then, works in men in such a way that their working is their own, yet He is involved in it. How is that? In this way, apparently. He is said to be working in us to will and to do. That would seem to mean that the Spirit, at work within the Christian soul, inclines it toward virtuous actions. The Holy Spirit resolves, and the virtuous human actions follow from this divine inspiration or influence. God does not do the work, but He disposes us to do it. Conversely, we do the work, but we do not dispose ourselves to it in the first place; He does that.

Thus there is a cooperation, or a divine-human partnership, in sanctification. Theologians and ethicists would use the term "synergistic" to describe it. Whereas justification, or the imputing of righteousness, is monergistic (that is, of God alone), sanctification, or the imparting of righteousness, is synergistic, or the work of God and man together.

This chapter has given us a hint of the divine Trinity's role in the saint's life. The Father, the person of the Godhead to Whom the saint addresses himself, holds the rights of the Godhead in the economic Trinity and is the executive of the divine policy. The Son is the Mediator between God and man, the one in Whose name prayers are presented and by Whose work they are rendered effectual. The Spirit, finally, moves the saint's heart toward God. He is called the Spirit of supplication because it is His presence in the souls of the redeemed that inclines them to call upon the Father in the name of the Son. Thus in each act of sincere prayer, devotion, and service the entire Trinity is involved.

Chapter 20

Propagation of the Faith

As I was driving to a speaking engagement, thinking about this chapter along the way, I saw a sign: "Eternity ahead—repent today—Jesus will save." That, I thought to myself, is propagation of the faith so that he who runs may read. It does not matter very much what the vehicle of expression may be, but Christianity demands expression. "A city that is set on a hill cannot be hid" (Matthew 5:14). Does a man "light a candle and put in under a bushel?" (Matthew 5:15). These things were not "done in a corner" (Acts 26:26). We must be prepared to give a reason for the hope that is within us (1 Peter 3:15). "Let the redeemed of the Lord say so" (Psalm 107:2). If we believe in our hearts we are to confess with our lips (Romans 10:9). If any man "confess Me before men, him will I confess also before My Father Which is in heaven" (Matthew 10:32).

Now this impulse to bear witness to others about Christ is not only a duty God lays upon the Christian, but a spontaneous impulse as well. His heart is filled with a goodly matter, his cup runneth over; what can he do but tell about it? Did you ever hear of any person on fire with anything about which he was able to remain silent? That is no doubt the thrust of Christ's reference to hiding a candle under a bushel. It is no more preposterous to light a candle and then hide it than it is to have Christ in the soul and then be silent about it.

If, therefore, a person says he loves Jesus and proceeds to keep it a secret, he must be a liar. He could not
keep it a secret if he loved a girl; surely he cannot keep it
secret that he loves, and is loved by, the Son of God. In
the nature of the case this is unthinkable; it is far more
plausible that the man is a liar than that such love would
not be expressed.

So it is not surprising when Christ says that, if a person does not confess Him before men, He will not confess
that person before His Father in heaven (Matthew 10:33).
That may seem contrary to Christian principles—more
like an eye for an eye and a tooth for a tooth. It is really
not that sort of thing, however. Christ's confession before
the Father is His statement on behalf of those who are His
and who love Him. Christ is simply inferring that a person who preferred life over confessing Him did not really
love Him, and that therefore Christ cannot confess him
before the Father as one of His.

This impulse to witness to Christ is not only the
product of duty and spontaneous affection for Christ, but
it is also motivated by a love for those to whom one witnesses. The Christian, knowing the joy of his salvation,
wants to bring the same joy to others. Knowing the
emptiness of his life without Christ, he can sympathize
with those who do not know Christ. Common decency
constrains him to share the fortune he has found with the
utterly destitute friends about him. Christianity begets a
generous spirit in its adherents, so that once they get it
they must share it. However niggardly and miserly a person may have been before conversion, he will feel differently afterwards. There is born in the soul, in the very
act of conversion, a new spirit to share the fruits of that

conversion. If he does not have that disposition, he does not have the Christian disposition, for if he tried to keep this gospel to himself it would be a fire in his bones that he could not stand.

Even though the believer's impulse to propagate his faith comes from a Christlike love for his fellow men, they may not necessarily appreciate it. It may be natural for the newborn to desire that others should know the same joy, but these others may prefer their present misery. Or they may like the notion of having the exuberant joy their friend has found, but they may not like the way he found it. After all, this follower of Christ must, as he says, deny himself and follow Christ. Now denial of *things*— giving up this or that for a short while—may be about the limit of the natural man's endurance. This notion of denying his *very self*, so that he becomes the slave of another and has no further will of his own but to do this other's will, may not at all appeal to a self-centered individual. He may find the joy set before him attractive, but not the cross by which it is reached. Accordingly, he may prefer to dispense with the joy itself in order to avoid the onerous cross.

So this person receiving his friend's witness may begin to rationalize, saying to himself: "Now I do not want this cross, though the joy is acceptable enough. But I cannot simply say I do not want the cross. That seems neither polite nor sporting. After all, this man insists it is a duty, and I can't deny that he has a point there. So I cannot simply flatly reject the doing of duty. At the same time I cannot accept this notion either. So let me present a more feasible ground for rejection."

He then says to his friend the evangelist, "Now look here, friend, I am glad that you have found something that means a great deal to you. And I do appreciate the fact that you are kind enough to want to share it with me. Don't think I am ungrateful. I do appreciate your kindness. But, you see, I already have a religion of my own that serves my purposes quite satisfactorily."

The evangelist may reply, "And what is that religion, may I ask?"

Friend: "Well, it is not exactly a religion in the usual sense of the word. But I believe in God, and I believe that if a person follows his conscience and does what he thinks is right, he and God will be on good terms. That is my belief, and I find it quite adequate. I have no objection to your religion—for you. If you find joy in believing all those things, then go on believing them. I affirm other people's right to believe as they wish. You let me believe what I want to believe, and I shall be happy to let you go on enjoying your faith."

Evangelist: "But, my friend, if I knew there was a bomb under your chair and you did not think so, would I be expected simply to affirm my belief in freedom of thought and let the matter rest there—or, more precisely, not rest there? Am I to go away saying, 'All right, my friend prefers to believe there is no bomb, so I must let him go on thinking that until he discovers by experience that there is a bomb'?"

Friend: "Come now, I am not sitting on any moral or religious bomb. You know that. To continue the analogy, I am simply sitting in a different chair from you, but both of us are safe. Now I am not interfering with where you sit; why don't you let me do what I want?"

Evangelist: "Well, of course, I shall have to permit you to stay where you are if you insist. If there were a bomb under your chair and you refused to believe it, I would

knock you out, carry you away, and let you watch the
explosion from a safe distance. But I cannot do that with
your religious convictions, for they must be voluntary if
they are to be of any value at all. But because you do
have something far more terrible than a bomb under you,
and since there is no way you can see this but by letting
me attempt to show you, I wish you would let me try.
What harm is there in my just talking to you? You don't
have to believe what I say; all I would like is an opportunity to tell you why what I say is true. You don't contend that what I say is not true; perhaps you even admit
it is true. And if there is even a possibility of its being
true, in which case you are even now sitting on an eternal
bomb which could go off at any minute, is it not sensible
for you just to listen to me until you are sure whether I
am wrong or right?"

Friend: "Listen, this is all tommy-rot. There are no
moral bombs. I am not in any such danger as you say. All
I want is to be left alone. Now why don't you go away and
believe what you want, and let me believe what I want."

Evangelist: "Very well, I shall go away."

Friend: "Thank God, that fanatic has left. These people
who think they are God Almighty and know everything
and that everybody else must go their way or be damned,
they make me weary. I hope that crank doesn't bother me
any more with that gospel of his. My motto is to live and
let live. Not a bad religion either, it seems to me. As a matter of fact, I wish these Christians would practice it."

Now this man is quite typical of those who are ap-
proached on behalf of the Christian religion. Not all, of
course, scoff at the witness and resent the doctrine, but
many do. Since no one, Christians included, enjoys being
treated as an unwelcome bore when he is trying do a

person the greatest conceivable good, he must reappraise
the situation and ask again if he indeed has any obligation
to interfere with the ways of the present world. Why not
let men think what they want?

Because this is the crassest nonsense and the greatest
possible folly. Men should believe the truth, not whatever they may want to believe. It is truth that does good,
not fiction. God is the one to be worshiped, not the idols
of men's minds.

Yes, the objection continues, but truth can come only
as men are willing to receive it, and if they are not willing
they will not receive it, no matter how earnestly, prayer-
fully, and convincingly it is presented. So why not let
men go to perdition in their folly, since we really cannot
do anything about it? It will do no good to compel them
to come in, for if we compel them they will not really come
in but only appear to do so. Faith is of the heart, so if
their hearts will not be persuaded—if they will not even
listen to Christian propaganda—why should the witness
continue as a *persona non grata*?

In answering this objection, we do not intend to suggest that Christians have an obligation to make deliberate
fools out of themselves and force their well-intentioned
apologetics on unwilling ears. Nevertheless, the duty of
witnessing wherever there is any possibility whatsoever
of gaining a hearing continues, because faith comes by
hearing and only by hearing. Granted, men will never, if
left to themselves, believe the gospel of Jesus Christ and
come to God through Him, for no man "cometh to Me except the Father Which sent Me draw him: and I will raise
him up at the last day" (John 6:44). If left to themselves
they will reject message and messenger alike. But God
does not always leave men to themselves; on the con-

trary, He sometimes changes their hearts, enlightens their minds, and renews their wills so that they who at first scoffed at the witness come to believe him. As Paul says to Timothy, "In meekness instructing those that oppose themselves; if God peradventure will give them repentance to the acknowledging of the truth" (2 Timothy 2:25). Whether men will believe or not is a "peradventure" of God. Left to themselves, they will not believe, but "peradventure" God will not leave them to their folly. He may always justly do so, but often, graciously, He does not do so.

But, the objector may continue, since the fruitfulness of this witness depends on whether God acts savingly or not, why do we not leave this matter entirely to God? Since our witness, as such, can never do anything but harden persons even more, and since, without the witness of God accompanying it, it will do no good, why not leave this business of converting souls to the one who actually does convert them?

For this reason: this matter is *not* simply left to God alone (although the premises the objector has just stated are true), because God does not exercise His sovereign prerogative except by means of the witness of His servants. They cannot convert anybody without Him, but He does not convert anybody without them. So whether men receive or reject the message, the Christian will continue his witness, by prayer, speech, action, or any other legitimate and sensible method. He may be the "savor of life unto life" for some and "of death unto death" for others (2 Corinthians 2:16). He may cause the darkness and the hardness of many souls to become still darker and harder, but he may also be the means of the softening and enlightening of others. Whether men hear or forbear, the witness's duty remains the same" to tell them, in any possible manner, of the truth of Christ which can save all who come to Him. Meanwhile the outcome of all is in God's hands—which is exactly where the witness wants it to be.

This discussion explains, incidentally, many other things. First, it explains why religion is caught as well as taught. That is, no matter how much truth is expounded, it will not be believed savingly unless God brings it home to the listener. However, though it cannot be caught merely by being taught, it must be taught first in order to be caught. Thus the role of Christian educators and evangelists is established, while at the same time all the prerogatives of heaven are guarded.

Furthermore, this sovereignty of God in conversion explains why some people "understand," or see the truth of Christianity, while others do not, even though those who see it may be far inferior in intelligence to those who do not. People are always asking why, if Christianity is true and there are sound arguments for it, those most capable of weighing arguments and understanding concepts do not accept it. Why are ordinary rather than extraordinary people the ones most likely to be convinced of the orthodox Christian faith? The answer is that persuasion of these things is not of flesh and blood, but of the Father in heaven (Matthew 16:17). That is, only as God removes the prejudice and carnality from the mind, only as He takes away the heart of stone and puts a heart of flesh in its place, will the darkened mind of man ever understand. And God is pleased to do this more often with the "babes" than with the "wise" of this world. "I thank Thee, O Father, Lord of heaven and earth, because Thou hast hid these things from the wise and prudent, and hast revealed them unto babes" (Matthew 11:25).

Third, we see why some men are so quickly persuaded and others so slowly, if at all. It is God Who makes the difference. He graciously reveals to some and not to others, and He reveals sooner to some and later to others.

So, then, it is our Christian duty to do three things. First, we must witness. Second, we must recognize that our witness can convince no one (regardless of its accuracy). Third, we must bow to the will of the sovereign God to use our witness as He will—to enlighten or to darken, to soften or to harden, to be a savor of life unto life or of death unto death.

Part 4

Objections Considered

Chapter 21

Are Morals Not Relative?

If nature is one, we would expect morals to be one. That is, if nature is the basis of morality, and if nature is the same at all times and in all places, we would expect no variation in the moral codes of mankind. If the nature is the same everywhere, then knowledge, and accordingly *conscientia*, would be the same also.

But on the other hand, if there is great variation among the people, climes, and times of mankind as far as moral judgment is concerned, must we not conclude that there is no conscience based on nature after all? If morals are relative to time and place, must not conscience be relative, and not an absolute law equally binding on all men?

Yes, if these latter contentions are true, we would have to admit that morals are relative. If nature's laws and revelations are universal, there should not be such differences among men. If such differences do indeed exist, we could only conclude that there is no fixed moral law such as we have tried to uncover in the previous chapters of this book. This objection, if sound, would be devastating. There is probably no more fundamental objection to morals that can be raised.

This objection is internally consistent; that is, if its premise (that there is this great variation in moral codes among humans) is true, then its conclusion (that there can be no such thing as fixed, absolute moral laws) would follow. But we challenge the premise; we challenge the data on which the objection rests. Or, more precisely, we challenge its interpretation of the data. As a matter of fact, we are deeply indebted to, and should acknowledge with appreciation, the great labors of those scholars who have amassed much evidence of the history of morals. We will challenge not their work, but the interpretation of the phenomena their erudite scholarship has uncovered.

In this chapter we will submit several considerations which, we believe, do not impugn the nature of the evidence under discussion but which do show some improprieties of interpretation. If our comments are sound, we will find that the data provide no basis for challenging the absoluteness of morals. We will here consider four explanations of the apparent relativism of morals: first, men sometimes wilfully refuse to think about their duty; second, sometimes they think, but onesidedly; third, sometimes they think wrongly; and fourth, sometimes they make wrong applications.

First, men sometimes refuse to think seriously about duty. May a man not blind himself to the law of nature and the voice of conscience without nature or conscience being to blame for his blindness? The law of nature, to give one clear example, favors marriage and opposes promiscuity, but a man desiring a woman who is not his wife may simply refuse to think about any moral deterrents. He is going to have this woman, right or wrong. His mind will not stop thinking, of course, but his preoccupation with passion will drown all considerations of conscience out of his thinking. If this can happen in the heat of passion, it can happen in all other situations. And if it can happen in one man, it can happen in many men, indeed in whole cultures. Their refusal to acknowledge a duty does not disprove the existence of the duty.

A second explanation of apparent moral relativism is that men sometimes give only onesided consideration to ethical matters. They may still think about such matters, but only in "loaded" fashion; that is, they may study the question, but only selected aspects of the question. They may be sound as far as they go, but they may deliberately go only far enough to justify a desired course of action, not far enough to reach a sound conclusion.

To illustrate this onesided ethical thinking, let us consider the "mercy killer." This is how such a person justifies his violation of the sixth commandment. First of all, he reasons that his heart is in the right place. What he does, he does because he loves people. He knows that one essential aspect of a moral duty is that it be motivated by love. He has love, and therefore he is moral so far.

Next, he knows there is more to morality than motive; there is the nature of the act itself. This too he finds to be right, for several reasons. For starters, the victim is in misery, and the killer will terminate this misery. As a result of his act, the sufferer will suffer no more. Furthermore, there is no "hope" for the sufferer; the doctors see no prognosis but eventual death. So, the killer concludes, he is doing only what nature is going to do anyway, and whereas nature is unconstrained by any feeling, the killer is constrained by feelings of compassion and can be more beneficent in doing what nature by itself would do without beneficence. Finally, the killer applies the Golden Rule to his action and determines that, in killing such sufferers, he is doing only what he would want them to do to him were he in their condition and they in his.

All in all, then, the mercy killer's act seems as good to

him as his motive. He is doing only what nature would do anyway, in a humane and moral manner, according to the highest ethical ideals.

As we evaluate the mercy killer, let us begin with the act and work backwards to the motive. What of the victim's suffering? There is no question that the person is suffering, perhaps excruciatingly. But does the mercy killer think that suffering, as such, justifies killing? No, he does not, or else he would kill the whole human race, all of whom suffer at one time or another. He would not even feel justified in killing all who suffer "excruciatingly," for this would still involve slaughtering a considerable number of persons.

So he must rest his case on the supposed hopelessness of this specific suffering. But does he really know it is hopeless? The doctors may not "see" any grounds for hope, but they would be the first to tell him of thousands of persons who have survived when their physicians had seen no grounds for hope. So a particular physician's loss of hope and "hopelessness" are obviously two vastly different things, and the argument from hopelessness also fails to support mercy killing.

What of the application of the Golden Rule to this case? The killer means that if he were in a condition of hopeless suffering, of which there could be no possible outcome but certain, excruciating, agonizing death, he would want his life to be terminated earlier and more easily. But since it has not been proved that this is actually the case, the situation is fundamentally changed. Beyond that, there is the question of how a man will feel in a given future situation that he has not yet experienced. It can be questioned how certainly a person in the bloom of health can know how he will feel when in the shadow of possible death. When actually in the shadow of death, he may feel quite differently.

What, finally, of the mercy killer's motive? We do not need to probe it. Even if it were good, this would not make the act good. On the contrary, if the act were wrong, then the motive of love would dictate that the person change his contemplated action.

In summing up, we can observe that the mercy killer has engaged in thinking, but onesidedly. Had he gone on to consider the whole situation more adequately, he would not have maintained the conclusion he reached on the basis of partial consideration. The bearing of all this on the argument for moral relativism seems clear. One may say that mercy killing is a virtue while the majority deem it a vice. This does not mean the action is morally relative; it means nothing more than that its advocates have not thought far enough. Incidentally, in this particular case we have tried to describe all the major arguments adduced in support of mercy killing, while submitting in reply only a few of the arguments opposed to it.

The third explanation of apparent moral relativism is that men sometimes make wrong judgments, which lead to wrong ethical standards. That is, they inaccurately apprehend the facts and therefore are wrongly convinced about the moral character of these facts. They think a certain thing is so, and their consciences react in a certain way, but if they recognized their factual error their consciences would react differently.

Let us take cannibalism as an example. Some tribes have regarded cannibalism as a duty, while the great majority of mankind considers it grossly immoral. Thus, this behavior is moral among one people but immoral among others. How could this be if the law of nature and conscience is the same for all peoples at all times?

Before we discuss how some peoples have attempted to justify cannibalism, let us think a moment about why mankind generally considers it immoral. Is it not because nature is good, obviously adapted to the needs of men, and thereby indicates its intention that men should live and prosper? Does not prospering entail peace and fraternity among men, inasmuch as the opposite would lead to the destruction of men and therefore the frustration of nature's purposes? Thus killing in any form is seen to be against nature and cannibalism, the most gruesome form of killing, appears to be all the more immoral. This is obvious to any thinking person, and accordingly the sanctity of human life has been enshrined in the law codes of virtually all mankind.

Why, then, do cannibals see it differently? In some instances they suppose other men to be their enemies, bent on destroying them. Killing these men becomes a duty, because they are murderers, and murderers violate the law of nature and existence. (We are not saying their judgment that the other men are intent on killing them is true, but simply that it is sometimes their judgment.) They believe they must kill or be killed, and therefore it becomes their duty to kill the potential murderer.

But why devour him? Why the gruesome method? This may warn other would-be murderers to desist from their nefarious purposes. It may be seen as only fair punishment for the unjustifiable enmity the victim had exhibited. Or, horrid as the thought may be, this may be seen as a perfectly natural way to dispose of the body while at the same time bringing an additional benefit to the tribe. If the person must be killed, they may contend, what harm is there in benefiting most fully from his execution?

It appears that in most cases, if not all, cannibalism is associated with religion. It is seen as the will of the deities. The victim may be viewed as a sacrifice to the god. Once again, we are not here evaluating whether this judgment is right, but simply making the point that if these persons suppose that their god wills such a rite, they will not be abandoning confidence in the law of nature, but simply recognizing that it is superseded by the god of nature. Their action would thus cease to be immoral in their minds, even if it ran counter to the general law of nature, for the god responsible for this general law would now be seen as making a specific exception to his law which must take precedence over the general. Therefore this command must be obeyed, on moral grounds. To do so would not violate the law of nature, for the law of nature is observed ultimately, because it is the law of the deity. And in this case the deity is directing otherwise. To refuse to obey the deity, were he to reveal his special will, would in fact be a refusal to obey the law of nature, for the law of nature is nothing but the law of the deity.

It may be extremely difficult for persons not accustomed to such bizarre patterns of thought even to imagine them, let alone understand them. However, if we are to understand anything about anyone we must enter that person's frame of reference—seeking not necessarily to agree with it, but merely to understand it. When we enter the heathen's frame of reference we discover that our difference is not over basic moral principles, which remain the same, but on matters of fact and judgment.

The cannibal is not denying the law of nature; he is simply supposing (wrongly, we know) certain factors that we do not admit. He agrees with us that, according to the general law of nature, a man should not kill another, much less devour him. We agree with him that if a person seeks to kill you without reason, you have a right to defend yourself, even if that means taking his life. Furthermore (although this is hard for us to admit theoretically), we also agree with the cannibal that if God demanded that we kill and devour another human being, we would have a moral obligation to do so.

There is, then, basic agreement, not disagreement, between cannibals and other men as to the fundamental laws of morals. Where do they differ? They differ with respect to specific judgments of fact. The cannibal says that certain men are his natural enemies, intent on killing him. He thinks himself justified in killing these persons simply because he believes they are his enemies. And he thinks it is God's will that he should offer this victim as a sacrifice. We do not admit these facts. But—and this is the crucial matter—if we did admit these facts, we would be cannibals, and if the cannibal did not believe these to be facts he would not be a cannibal. We and he are both operating on the same moral principles, which are the same without regard to people, place, or time. If we saw the facts alike, we would act the same.

Let us briefly mention the fourth faulty basis for moral relativism: wrong application of the right moral law. For example, the *lex talionis*, or law of retaliation, is a sound law often unsoundly applied. It belongs to serious cases, of the sort that deserve to come before the tribunals of men and nations. It requires an eye for an eye and a tooth for a tooth; that is, it dictates that justice consists in fitting the punishment to the crime, so that it may be neither too severe nor too lenient. All men recognize this law and make it a staple of their jurisprudence, and God confirms it by special revelation.

But there is a common, wrong application of this law. Some suppose that it is to be applied not just to serious cases but to all cases, and not only in our courts and tribunals but between individuals. Thus these people a develop a litigious spirit and a spiteful disposition. They are never happy unless they are bearing a grudge or getting even. Every slight must be avenged; nothing can be overlooked.

That such cannot be a legitimate application of this legitimate law is clear not only from special revelation (Matthew 5:38–42) but from natural law as well. It is readily evident that if everyone were to get even for everything, life in this world would be an unending, unbroken series of private wars between every man and his neighbor. This, all men know, nature does not intend.

When, therefore, we see an apparent moral deviation or relativism, we may conclude that some difference in judgment, not in the moral quality of human thinking, is actually responsible for this aberration. We are reminded of the astronomer who noticed that the planet he was studying did not move in its regular orbit. He knew there must be some factor to explain this, for nature produced uniformity; if this orbit did not appear uniform, some other body must be attracting the planet out of orbit. Making the computations necessary to estimate the size and distance of the unknown body which could cause this deviation, the astronomer was able to turn his telescope and discover a new planet. Similarly, examining differences among humans will lead us to understand better the reasons for these differences, but it will not lead us, if we handle the facts properly, to the philosophy of moral relativism.

Chapter 22

Are Bible "Morals" Not Sometimes Immoral?

It is usually believed that the Bible is the fundamental source not only of Western civilization but especially of our moral theories. However, some think the Bible is also the source of some immorality, as in the case of the modern pastor who attributed the crime wave to Scripture. We must address this common category of objections.

First of all, let us distinguish carefully between recording something and sanctioning it. Not everything recorded in the Bible is approved by the Bible. The Bible is not morally responsible for every behavior it relates. This fact should be obvious to all. No historian would want to be held responsible for the murders, rapes, thefts, or other vices his narrative faithfully records, and we do not hold him responsible for anything except the accuracy of his report. Likewise, the Bible relates many events as having occurred without necessarily giving any stamp of approval to them.

This distinction may seem so obvious as to be unnecessary, but the subsequent discussion will show that it is sometimes forgotten. Many of the moral objections raised against the Bible can be answered by applying this distinction between relating something and sanctioning it.

Thus, for example, it is sometimes said that the Bible taught, at one time, that polygamy was legitimate. The Bible did indeed describe this practice as prevailing even among godly men. But this is not the same thing as sanctioning the practice, and nowhere does the Bible sanction it.

Again, the Bible relates that the divorce laws were more lax at one time than at another. However, all Christ says is that Moses suffered the Jews of his day to put away their wives for causes less than infidelity (Matthew 19:8). This is not the same as saying that Moses sanctioned the practice. He may have permitted something, in the sense of not having forbidden it, for one reason or another without having given his positive approval of it.

Again, the Bible seems to glorify lying when it tells of the Hebrew midwives who lied in order to save the Hebrew male children. We have already discussed the moral problems pertaining to the eighth commandment. Here it is sufficient to say that the Bible only relates that they did this and why; it then approves *why* they did it, but not *that* they did it. It is possible for a person to do a bad deed with a good motive, and to have his motive commended but not the deed. The Bible also says that Abraham lied about his wife; it does not say that he did rightly in so speaking. As a matter of fact, these cases illustrate the candor and, as we might call it today, "realism" of the Bible in presenting an honest, unvarnished account of the lives of its saints. No one gets the impression from real life that godly persons are without faults, and the Bible does not give that impression either. At the same time, in its didactic sections (as distinguished from its historical parts), it condemns these blemishes, even in the saints.

Having made these general remarks, we will confine ourselves within this chapter to only two, but probably the greatest two, specific objections against the morality of the Bible: its commands to kill "innocent" persons and its doctrine of hell.

Is the Bible not immoral in sanctioning violations of the sixth commandment? Does it not merely condone killing but actually command it at times? Does it not even command the killing of children, innocent children? Does it not even represent God Himself as killing people, and then even as killing them eternally in hell?

We have already insisted that the Bible teaches capital punishment, and we have defended the morality of that teaching in our discussion of the sixth commandment. But capital punishment relates only to individuals. Wars and mass extermination, while they differ only in degree and not in principle, still are so often singled out as objections to the Bible that we ought to consider them here. Nevertheless, we must repeat that if the execution of one person may be justified, the execution of many persons may be justified. There is no reason why the ethical principle in question cannot hold simply because a large number of persons are involved.

Someone may demur at this point: "Granted that if one person may be justifiably executed, so may a whole city or nation of persons. But there is a complicating factor in the bigger picture that is not present in the smaller one. There may be innocent people in a whole city, may there not? As a matter of fact, is it not very likely that there are innocent persons in such a large group? Indeed, may we not even be certain that there will be one group of innocent persons, namely the infants? These could not possibly have had any part in crime and therefore should not have any part in the punishment inflicted for the crime, as would be the case were they executed along with the adults, all of whom may conceivably be guilty."

Let us assume we are at war with a city because of certain atrocities that city has committed. We must admit that there may be individuals in the city who took no part in the atrocities. We must also admit that there may be persons who did not approve of the atrocities, or who even did everything they could to prevent them. These persons may even be in the city's prison for trying to stop the commission of these atrocities. These persons, then, we admit, should not be destroyed by our armies.

But if we drop any bombs or shoot any guns against the city, we may kill the innocent persons. What are we to do? Drop no bombs and shoot no guns, because we may kill some innocent persons? If we did thus refrain we would permit this city to continue committing atrocities. Can we do this? Well, it would come down to the question of whether we would kill more innocent persons by attacking this city than we would permit to be killed if we did not attack it. We would also have to consider that those innocent persons in the city had guilt in one sense that the innocent victims outside the city did not have: they were citizens of that city and, therefore, part of its life and government even though they were not in agreement on this particular policy. Furthermore, the offenders of that city who deserve to suffer would suffer somewhat in the harm done to the innocent people in their city. This same statement could not be made about the harm done to the innocent people outside the city.

In view of these considerations, we will have to admit that, under circumstances where far more harm would be done to innocent persons by refraining from attacking a city than by attacking it, the army would have to attack and could be legitimately exonerated for any deaths it unavoidably inflicted on innocent persons in that city. But,

at the same time, it would not be exonerated for killing innocent people where this could have been avoided. What
has been stated here would, presumably, apply to infants
as well as to other innocent persons in the city.

"Yes," someone replies, "but this still does not exonerate some of the biblical destructions because they were
carried out against 'innocent' persons such as babies
when these could have been saved from the disaster.
Indeed," the objector may continue, "God specifically
commanded the Israelites on several occasions to kill every man, woman, and child. This was surely a divine
command to kill the innocent, was it not? Did we not say
above that if an army went in to attack a city it had a
moral obligation to save the innocent if it could? Here,
then, is such an occasion, and God specifically commands
the army not to save the innocent."

The objector, however, is overlooking one significant
point. Our modern armies do not have divine guidance
when they go to destroy a city; the Israelites did. So far as
we know, some persons in such a city may be innocent;
but God may know far differently. If, therefore, God knew
that all were worthy of death and commanded an army to
administer this punishment, there could be no legitimate
objection, could there?

"Yes," the objector responds again, "we have just said
that babies could not possibly be guilty of complicity in
the crimes for which our army would be destroying the
city. Neither could the babies conceivably be guilty of
the crimes for which the Israelites, under God's direction,
were destroying the city. If the child was innocent, even
God could not call him guilty; and if he did not deserve to
die even God could and would not say that he did deserve
to die."

Granted that God could not call someone guilty who was innocent. But do we know that children are innocent? We know they are innocent of a particular crime, to be sure, but do we know that they have no guilt at all? Do we know that they are born without guilt—that there was no representative guilt? Are we sure that no one had stood probation for them and had failed and brought judgment upon all for whom he stood probation, just as the Bible itself says Adam did?

"All right," the objector continues, "that is possible. Maybe the child is guilty and deserving to die. But surely he is not guilty of the crime for which a particular city is being destroyed."

We reply that if God devotes any city to destruction it is because of sin. Does it make any difference what sin? Or, again, if the city is being destroyed for a particular sin or sins, and some persons are destroyed who are not guilty of that particular sin, are they the victims of injustice if they are guilty in their own right and deserve to die anyway?

There is only a problem here, in reality, if children are thoroughly innocent. If they are not completely innocent, then there can be no true objection against their punishment. To state it positively, we may say that the destruction of infants at God's command is a tacit indication that children *are* guilty persons, for otherwise God would not thus proceed. We do not know with certainty that they are *not* guilty, and the fact that God punishes them as if they were guilty would lead us to believe that they *are* guilty.

But now the objector declares, "This is very difficult to accept. It seems an outrage to all our notions of justice." But is it really? We know that children have colic before they reach the age of accountability, and colic causes excruciating suffering. Other children are born with far greater disabilities than colic, although they have done nothing right or wrong, indeed nothing moral at all. And we know full well that millions of infants have died. Nature has not hesitated to inflict this ultimate punishment upon children. If nature is under the control of God, as we believe, then God by natural revelation, as well as by special revelation, teaches that children are guilty and deserving of punishment.

We have shown that children are deserving of God's punishment, but that does not mean they deserve our punishment. They may have sinned against God but not man; in this case God may justifiably bring judgment upon them as they are, but man may not. Therefore, an army must discriminate between the innocent and the guilty when it destroys a city, unless it has specific direction from God, as is supposed in the case before us.

Someone may accuse us of begging the question. The Bible is charged with immorality because it allegedly teaches that God commands the death of innocent persons, and we are defending it by saying that God can do no wrong. Yes, this is what we are saying—and in doing so we are not begging the question at hand. If God does command a particular slaughter and God can do no wrong, then that slaughter was justified and the Bible is exonerated. If the objector wishes to ask whether the Bible was right in saying God commanded this, that is another question entirely. We cannot be accused of begging the question before us—namely, whether the Bible's teaching can be defended on moral grounds—just because we have not answered a different question which is not before us. We have attempted to address this other ques-

tion—whether the Bible is the Word of God and histori-
cally accurate—elsewhere in this volume and more fully
in the companion volume, *Reasons for Faith*. Here we are
assuming the Bible's veracity and are dealing with the
question of whether the destruction of whole cities puts
God in an immoral light and therefore reflects adversely
on the Bible which teaches this. Our answer is that it does
not, for God may know, indeed may be presumed to
know, things about persons which men do not know. For
this reason, the fact that the Bible says babies are guilty
and worthy of death is not a proof of the immorality of the
Bible.

Some objectors, even if willing to grant all the above,
will still raise the second classic objection: hell. Granted
that sin must be punished, perhaps even by death, and
that God has the right to do so or to command others to
carry out this punishment, nevertheless does even God
have the right to inflict hell upon any finite being? That
is, may He punish eternally those who sin only in this
temporal world? We have faced this question in the previous volume, so we will borrow part of that discussion
here.

The God of the Bible is represented as an eternally
glorious being, the only ultimately good, worthy, and excellent sovereign of heaven and earth. If it is important
for men to maintain the dignity of men, to respect those
in authority, to honor father and mother, or to fear the
king, it is infinitely more important for God to maintain
the dignity of the Godhead. If we cannot permit men to
cast aspersions on our mother or on anyone we respect,
it is an inconceivably greater evil to dishonor the majesty
of heaven.

If we are aware of the awesome nature of this evil, God

must be infinitely more aware of it. Suitable punishment for infractions against the honor of God is not only proper and necessary, but failure to deliver such punishment would be a tacit abnegation by God of His glory and majesty. This would be unthinkable. In other words, so far from punishment for sin being a petty action, it is the essential action of infinite majesty. It is precisely because God is great, not because He is small, that He must maintain the glory of His name.

Those who claim Scripture itself opposes the vengeance of God usually argue this point from the Bible's representation of the divine being as infinitely good and merciful. The Bible does indeed frequently teach this truth. Mercy is a distinguishing attribute of the God of Scripture, and "God is love" (1 John 4:8). However, God has many other attributes as well. The Bible relates and interconnects these various attributes; it does not separate them. It is precisely because men disregard God's love and presume upon God's mercy that God's glory and majesty call for suitable reprisal. It is a great sin to dishonor the mercy and love of God. No sin can be committed with impunity, and certainly not a sin so heinous and odious as that of despising the very love which offers the forgiveness of sin.

Psalm 95 begins with a most cordial invitation to come and worship God, and it closes by contemplating those who harden their hearts, warning them that God will swear in His wrath that they shall not enter into His rest. "How," asks the New Testament, "shall we escape if we neglect so great salvation?" (Hebrews 2:3). Jesus said it would be tolerable for Sodom and Gomorrah in comparison with Chorazin and Bethsaida in the day of judgment, referring to the fact that they had spurned so much more of the goodness and mercy of God than had the perverse Sodomites. If God's love and mercy were exposed to be despised by men, and if men could go on to despise all the other attributes of God because they could presume on that mercy, this would utterly subvert the whole moral order, make God the slave of men, put a premium on vice, and make hell into heaven and heaven into hell. In short, if men could presume on the mercy of God, that would put God at the mercy of men.

Chapter 23

Does Salvation by Grace Not Undermine Morals?

We have considered criticisms of some specific moral positions of the Bible. This is a somewhat piecemeal attack. Others, however, object at a more fundamental point. They lay the axe at the root of the trees, not satisfied with merely trimming the branches. They object to the very underlying theory of the Bible from which its ethical implications proceed. They object to its very doctrine of salvation by grace through faith; or, more particularly, they object to its scheme of salvation by grace through faith apart from works or without works.

This gratuitous salvation, they say, must necessarily undermine all incentive to morals. If salvation is based on something other than works, indeed on something opposite to works, where do works or moral deeds come in? Do they not rather go out? If a person believes in salvation without works it will be a sin for him to offer works for his salvation. Will he not, therefore, be indifferent to good deeds, or even positively hostile to them? If so, then Christianity is not only unsympathetic to morals, but actually hostile to them, and a good Christian will in fact be a libertine (one who is indifferent to morals) or even an antinomian (one who is against the moral law).

This is no new objection to Christianity. It was presented and answered in biblical times. Thus Paul mentions

212

those who accused him of teaching that we should sin all the more so that grace may abound more (Romans 5:20–21). "Shall we continue in sin that grace may abound?" he describes his critics as asking. And again, he denies that he makes the law "of none effect" (Galatians 3:17). James apparently wrote the second chapter of his epistle to deal with this objection.

Let this be said at the outset: Christianity's teaching on salvation by grace is no more clear than its insistence that its adherents live godly lives in Christ Jesus. Whatever problems, if any, may arise from this fact, it cannot be denied (nor do the critics deny) that Christianity does require its followers to be moral persons. Christ Himself said, "If any man will come after Me, let him deny himself, and take up his cross, and follow Me" (Matthew 16:24). "If ye love Me," He said on another occasion, "keep My commandments" (John 14:15). He cursed the fig tree because it had leaves which were supposed to indicate the presence of fruit which it did not have. He commanded His disciples to let their "light shine before men that they may see your good works, and glorify your Father Who is in heaven" (Matthew 5:16). Indeed, Christ commanded those who came after Him to be "perfect even as your Father in heaven is perfect" (Matthew 5:48). If anyone wanted to avoid being cast into hell, he must be prepared (morally speaking) to cut off his hand and pluck out his eyes (Matthew 5:29–30). And they must continue this rigorous living to the end if they wished to be considered His disciples and be saved (Matthew 16:25).

Likewise Paul, the great champion of justification by faith alone, said that if he ceased to beat his body he would be a castaway (1 Corinthians 9:27). He warned all thieves, fornicators, idolaters, drunkards, and other gross offenders that they would not inherit the kingdom of God, with no exceptions (1 Corinthians 6:9–10). "God is not mocked," he wrote, "for whatsoever a man soweth, that shall he also reap. For he that soweth to his flesh shall of the flesh reap corruption; but he that soweth to the Spirit shall of the Spirit reap life everlasting" (Galatians 6:7–8).

Indeed, this is the teaching of the entire Bible, Jesus and Paul, Old Testament and New. We hardly need go on multiplying texts. We assume no one doubts that the Bible upholds the moral law and requires conformity to it. Even the objectors do not question this.

The objection is as follows. Granted that the Bible explicitly teaches moral duty and requires Christians to practice it, is this consistent with its doctrine of salvation by grace through faith? It says that men may not boast of their works, because they are saved by grace. Still it requires these works, as we have seen. Is there not manifest inconsistency here? If salvation is by grace alone, without works, how can the Bible require them? Does Paul not write, "Now to him that worketh not, but believeth on Him that justifieth the ungodly, his faith is counted to him for righteousness" (Romans 4:5)? How, then, can the Bible consistently avoid antinomianism? Or, if it does avoid this tendency, how does it maintain its doctrine of salvation by grace alone through faith?

In this objection the crucial word is not any of the big terms but an insignificant, often unnoticed one. The misunderstanding does not rest on the meaning of faith, works, or justification, but upon the preposition "without" or "apart from." The objector is unconsciously understanding this preposition differently from its meaning in the Bible, as we shall attempt to show. The objector is supposing that "without" in the expression "justification by faith without works" means "without *any* connection with." That is, he thinks the Bible is teaching justification by faith without this faith having any connection with works. Thus he supposes that the Bible represents it as possible that a man may have faith, so as to be justified, and thenceforth do no good works yet remain a justified person.

Based on this construction of the doctrine, the objector has every reason to object with all possible vigor and moral abhorrence. If this were what the Bible taught, there could be no question that its doctrine was the death of all morality. If this were its theology, it would indeed be a profound mystery that the Bible then turned around and taught moral obligation to its adherents.

Now this interpretation of the word "without" is not the only possible one. It could mean without any connection in one sense, but not necessarily without any connection in another. Such a distinction is conceivable, at least. If this is the case, the Bible could legitimately be expected to make clear exactly in what sense it means "without." We think it does this.

Granting the theoretical possibility that the word "without," as used in the Bible, may rule out one particular kind of connection between faith and works, what is this particular kind? The answer is that "without" means without any connection in merit. The Bible's doctrine of justification by faith alone means this: the person who has faith in Christ alone is justified by the merit of Christ's redemption alone, without the believer contributing any merit of his own to his justification. Jesus paid it all, and the person who is saved, or justified, ac-

cepts the payment of Christ and on that basis alone is accepted by God as a righteous person. At this point the
believer's own works, if he has any, make no contribution
at all. For that reason there is no room for boasting. All is
of God, without any help from man.

To return to Paul's expression, "Now to him that worketh not but believeth on him that justifieth the ungodly,
his faith is counted to him for righteousness" (Romans
4:5). Notice that the justified person is without works
("worketh not"), that he is represented as one that "believeth" on another ("on him that justifieth"), and that his
"faith" alone is "counted for righteousness." In Ephesians
2:10 Paul states that the justified are God's workmanship
in Christ Jesus. Christ says that when the publican who
could not so much as lift up his eyes to heaven confessed
that he was a sinner and pleaded for mercy, he went down
to his house justified (Luke 18:13–14).

But the Bible does not say this justified person has no
relation of any kind with works, or that his works have
no connection whatsoever with his faith. Having said un-
ambiguously that his works have no connection of a
meritorious kind with his faith and justification, it does
teach that there is an inextricable connection of another
kind. Works have an inseparable connection with faith as
fruit with root, as consequent with antecedent, as result
with cause.

We have already shown that the Bible teaches that
true Christians must do good works, or else they are not
true Christians. Let us now show the basis for this statement in its consistency with justification by faith alone.
The Bible says this because the type of faith that justifies
is of an active nature and, therefore, expresses itself. It is
a vital principle and, like all vital principles, gives birth to

vital expression. The expression of faith is in works.

Hebrews 11 states as something of a refrain, as it relates the various exploits of the heroes of the faith, that "by faith" they did such and such. All the mighty deeds therein mentioned are described as expressions of the faith these heroes had in their hearts and, therefore, exhibited in their deeds. On the other hand, the Bible never says, and indeed could not say, "By faith so-and-so did nothing," or "By faith so-and-so did evil." If someone did nothing or did evil, this was not a result of his faith. Persons who have this vital principle of faith still do evil things at times, but in spite of, and not because of, this principle. The principle itself leads persons to do the deeds which God, toward whom the faith is directed, commands to be done.

If "faith" does not produce good works, it is not faith at all. In James's words, it is "dead" (James 2:26). It does not exist. Faith, he says, reaches its goal (*telos*), or is made perfect, in works (James 2:22). Hence he says that we are justified by works (2:24), for one of two reasons. Either James means that we are justified in the sense of vindication (which is not an uncommon use of the word, either in biblical times or today), or he means that we are justified by works, in the sense that works are nothing but faith in action and simply show the reality of our trust in God. In this chapter James is showing the reality of Abraham's faith by his works, specifically by the work of offering up his son at the divine command. Having cited that example, James comes to the same conclusion as Paul concerning Abraham. Indeed, they cite the very same Old Testament text as proof: "Abraham believed God, and it was counted to him for righteousness" (Romans 4:3, James 2:23).

What James shows, in his way, of the vitality of true
faith, Paul shows in a different way, but both of them
agreeing completely. Says Paul: "Shall we continue in sin,
that grace may abound? God forbid. How shall we, that
are dead to sin, live any longer therein?" (Romans 6:1–2).
Do we destroy the law through faith? "God forbid. Yea, we
establish it" (Romans 3:31).

We may go over the same ground again for clarity,
using a different word as our guide. Consider now the use
of the word "necessary" in this discussion. Are works necessary for salvation, according to Christianity? Yes and
no. Yes, they are necessary in the sense that no one will
ever be saved without them, since no one will ever be
saved without faith and true faith is never without works.
No, they are not necessary in the sense that a person is
saved without contributing anything at all to the merit
upon which salvation is based.

Let us make the same point from another angle.
Christianity is neither legalism nor antinomianism, but it
includes the elements of truth from each without the elements of error in either. With legalism it agrees that
works are necessary, but against legalism it teaches that
these necessary works do not form the foundation or
meritorious ground of salvation. With antinomianism
Christianity agrees that men are not saved by works but
by grace alone through faith, but against antinomianism
it insists that saved persons must, with a necessity of
consequence, do good works.

Notice how Christianity combines joy and blessedness with anxiety and earnestness. If it produced joy and
blessedness without moral earnestness and striving, it
would not be good. If it produced moral earnestness and
striving without joy and blessedness, it would be grim.

Neither would seem fully natural. Man is made for blessedness and goodness, and either one of these without the other could not be the natural order. In a religion truly from heaven we would expect both blessedness and goodness. And both elements do truly appear in Christianity, as we see, for by faith men are made happy and blessed yet also introduced to genuine moral responsibility.

This word "faith" signifies coming to rest in and commune with the living God as a Savior, Friend, and Lord. At the same time, man is God's creature and God's servant, and therefore must obey Him and do His will; and for men in a fallen condition this will necessarily involve some moral striving and trembling. This too is present in the Christian plan of salvation; the Christian works out his salvation with fear and trembling, because he knows that true faith expresses itself in wholehearted and full conformity to the entire, exacting law of God. At the same time, therefore, that a Christian strives as far as possible to be perfect as his Father in heaven is perfect, he knows that his justification is by faith alone, apart from the works of the law. So he has all the earnestness of a person whose whole salvation could be thought to rest on morality, and all the joy of the person whose whole salvation rests on free grace.

We conclude, then, that Christianity, properly understood, is not against the strictest possible morality. Faith is not the enemy of morals, but its greatest friend—indeed an indispensable friend, for without faith no man can please God. How can any so-called good works be viewed with pleasure by God if they come from a heart that does not trust Him and His revelation? If they were good in any sense, how could they be good in His sight?

Rather, even the plowing of the wicked must indeed be evil (Proverbs 21:4), although the plowing in itself seems good enough.

Christianity is in fact the enemy of immorality in any manifestation. If Christianity opposes unbelief, it does not oppose immorality any less, because immorality is ultimately an expression of unbelief. Belief is expressed in morality. Piety of the truly Christian sort is never contrary to morals but, on the contrary, demands them, both explicitly and implicitly.

Chapter 24

What Shall We Say about
the "Good Works" of Non-Christians?

Probably the two strongest arguments against Christianity are the obnoxious Christian and the pleasing non-Christian. If "by their fruits ye shall know them," do not these two persons prove Christianity to be untrue? If Christianity were true, it should not produce obnoxious persons; and if it alone were true, how could pleasant persons be produced apart from it? We discussed the first of these problems, the hypocritical Christian, in the companion volume. Here let us face the other side of the same problem: the apparently "Christian" nonbeliever.

Let us confess at the outset the reasonableness of the contention. Admittedly there exist pleasing persons who are not Christians or even who actively oppose to Christianity. Augustine spoke of the "splendid vices" of the heathen in this context. The evident sincerity of some unbelievers is beyond doubt; in some cases this sincerity extends to martyrdom. There are men and women, not Christians, who exhibit great prayer, alms, self-denial, justice, and general morality.

At the same time, it is also fair and necessary to insist that such persons are the exception, not the rule. They are conspicuous because they are relatively few. While we will not deny their existence nor that there are a goodly number of them, we will still insist that they are relatively

few; that is, that such extraordinary outward morality
apart from Christian influence is unusual. For example, a
study was conducted on the contributions made to the
"community chest" of a certain Pennsylvania town after
the entire population was solicited for this general
benevolence fund. The study disclosed that more than 95
percent of the contributions were made by church members. In this discussion we are acknowledging the existence of the other 5 percent, but are also observing that
the overall percentage is not higher than that, if that
high.

The Bible also acknowledges the "good works" of the
unconverted. "Ye then," says Christ, "being evil know
how to give good gifts to your children" (Matthew 7:11).
Christ recognized that men, even while evil, did some
good things, such as giving gifts to their children. The
Bible acknowledges "natural affections," meaning that men
by nature, however, fallen, still have some respect for
their parents and family. The apostle Paul began his famous chapter on love with these words: "Though I speak
with the tongues of men and of angels, and have not
charity, I am become as sounding brass, or a tinkling
cymbal. And though I have the gift of prophecy, and understand all mysteries, and all knowledge; and though I
have all faith, so that I could remove mountains, and have
not charity, I am nothing. And though I bestow all my
goods to feed the poor, and though I give my body to be
burned, and have not charity, it profiteth me nothing"
(1 Corinthians 13:1–3). This statement shows that Paul
knew men were capable of great philanthropy, eloquence,
and martyrdom without having love—that is, without
being filled with the love of God.

In spite of these acknowledgments, the Bible considers

all these as works of the flesh (that is, of the unregenerate or unconverted nature of fallen man). It says of these persons that "in the flesh they cannot please God" (Romans 8:8). It says, as we noted at the end of the previous chapter, that "the plowing of the wicked is sin" (Proverbs 21:4). The Bible thus regards even legitimate and useful occupations, which are good in themselves, as being sin as far as the unconverted persons who do them are concerned. The Bible even states that the prayer of the wicked is an abomination to the Lord (Proverbs 15:8). This means the most holy and religious exercises of the unregenerate are obnoxious to God, worse than if they had not been done at all. Thus these things not only fail to qualify as virtues, but they are vices (however good and holy they may be in and of themselves) when done by fleshly persons.

Someone may wonder how this discussion relates to the biblical doctrine that "by their fruits ye shall know them" (Matthew 7:16), so we should address this point briefly before proceeding to show why the Bible so severely censures the "civic righteousness," as Luther called it, of the unconverted. The observations we have just made are not contrary to this teaching of Christ. He teaches that evil men will bring forth evil fruits or deeds, and we are saying exactly the same here. The deeds in question are only apparently or outwardly good, not truly good; they constitute no exception to the rule that men do not gather grapes from thistles. These only *seem* to be grapes, as we will show; they are not really such.

Still, a further truth arises here. The text says that "by their fruits *ye* shall know them." But how can we know the existence of false motives and hypocrisy? Probably we cannot detect the evil nature of apparently good works as God can (although we may often feel reasonably sure that that evil nature is lurking within), but no one says that hypocrites do nothing but seemingly good works that are actually bad. As a matter of fact, they also do bad works that are obviously bad, in addition to doing bad works that may outwardly appear to be good.

For example, the hypocrites may give good gifts to their children, but it may be quite apparent that they have no concern for those who are not their friends. An unconverted farmer may look honorable while working in the fields, but it is altogether possible that if we are able to peek at his behavior at home we will find that he is not so apparently virtuous there. Sometimes a man gives money to feed the poor, yet even as he does so it is apparent that he has no love for the poor, but is giving for some other, convenient reason. We have read of martyrs who were also very vain persons, and who while waiting for their death thoroughly enjoyed the adulation of the crowds. So, while, the thorns may be mixed with grapes, we can tell that the grapes do not belong to the same plant as the thorns. Christ's teaching about knowing men by their fruits appears in the context of a warning about false prophets, implying, apparently, that their doctrine will betray them also. Thus, if the unconverted do any simulated works of righteousness it will be evident that they attribute their so-called righteousness to some native virtue of their own and thus betray themselves.

But let us return from that exposition and come now to the central question of this chapter: why does the Bible condemn all the works of the wicked, no matter how good they may be in themselves, when objectively considered apart from the doer himself? First, it condemns men because their *motives* are evil. Love is the only acceptable motive for a good act. If an act appears to be good yet is done without love, it is not good. Indeed, if it appears to be good yet lacks love it is more evil than if it did not even appear to be good, for hypocrisy is sinful in both its lack of love and its pretense. Love must be without dissimulation. However good an act may appear to be, whether a display of great philanthropy ("though I give all my goods to feed the poor") or martyrdom ("though I give my body to be burned"), it profits nothing. Love, God says in Scripture, is the fulfilling of the law. And the whole law is summarized in this: "Thou shalt love. . . ."

This is the same as to say that the motive of an act must be God Himself. For God is love, and God acts in love. His decrees are dictated by this motive. Even the display of His wrath toward the wicked is motivated by His love for the elect, as it ultimately contributes to their greater happiness. He has no pleasure in the death of the wicked; He permits it, apparently, only for the pleasure He does find in the lives of the righteous which are heightened by contrast. So a good act is a God act, or a love act. Whatever other properties an act may have, if it lacks God it lacks good, and if it lacks love it lacks God.

Now the unconverted are utterly devoid of true love. This is apparent from the fact that love comes only from Christ and not from fallen nature. We love, the Apostle John teaches us, because He first loved us. Except as the love of the Holy Spirit has been shed abroad in our hearts, there is no love in our hearts. Again this is apparent because God is love, and where God is not (i.e., in the sinful heart), there love is not. It is the love of Christ that constrains us so that we may thus no longer live unto ourselves, but unto Him who died for us and rose again (2 Corinthians 5:14–15). And loving Him who is the

Head, we love the members of Christ's body also. When they are in prison we visit *Him* (by visiting them), and when they are hungry we feed Him by serving them food. But the unconverted do not visit or feed or give drink or clothing to Him, for they do not love Him. Therefore they shall be surprised to hear, at the last judgment, that they never visited Him or gave to Him, because they never saw Him at all. He was not in their hearts or thoughts. They did not love Him and could not love His members.

To be sure, the unconverted do, in a manner of speaking, love their friends and themselves. "If ye love them which love you, what reward have ye? do not even the publicans the same? And if ye salute your brethren only, what do ye more than others? do not even the publicans so?" (Matthew 5:46–47). But this is not true love for others; it is merely self-interest casting a shadow. "I love me and mine—my family, my friends. . . ." The heathens and publicans get no further because they have no true love. They love only themselves, as they see themselves reflected in those who are thought to benefit them.

The unconverted not only have no love in their heart, but they have positive hatred and nothing but hatred. They hate God, their neighbor, and even themselves (their true selves). Romans 5:10, referring to the preconversion state, says "when we were enemies. . . ." Men are hostile to God, and never more so than when they profess to resent that charge and insist that they love God. God Himself—and He ought to know—says they are His enemies. They are at war with Him. "The kings of the earth set themselves, and the rulers take counsel together against the Lord, and against His anointed" (Psalm 2:2). They destroy His prophets and at last kill His only Son, because the Son is the light and they hate the light, not only refusing to come to it but even attempting to put it out. "No man can serve two masters," said Christ, "for either you will love the one and hate the other . . ." (Matthew 6:24). The world serves the prince of this world and hates the Prince of Peace. If men could do so, they would kill God. He would not be safe in their hands for a moment.

It may not be obvious that natural men hate even their friends, whom they think they love. But consider, for example, a godless parent's behavior toward his son, whom he naturally professes to love. He does not teach the child that he by nature in a lost condition. He does not attempt to lead him to the Savior. Rather, he does the opposite. By example and teaching he resists the Spirit's working and keeps that child from the only true source of help. He thus makes his son twice as much a child of hell as himself. His very benefactions to the child do the most harm of all, because by giving him food, education, and the comforts of life the father tends to induce trust in his leadership, with the result that the child trusts his blind guide and both fall into the pit of hell. Part of hell's very hellishness will be the presence of godless children cursing their godless parents who led them there.

The natural man loves himself least of all. Everything he does, whether it influences others or not, is his action. And every action he does as a rebel against heaven simply treasures up more wrath against the day of wrath and the righteous judgment of God (Romans 2:5). Everything he does for himself in his impenitence and hardness is an act against himself. Every action he takes, in its purest selfishness, is suicidal. In his supreme attempt at self-interest, he utterly destroys himself. As Ecclesiastes 4:5

puts it, "The fool foldeth his hands together, and eateth his own flesh."

Second, the Bible condemns men because their *moral standard* is evil. The only proper standard for a creature must be the law of his Creator. The Creator Who gave him life must also be the regulator of that life. Since God sustains the creature at every moment, He has the right at every moment to expect the creature to obey Him. How can a young man keep his way clean? By giving heed unto God's law. This law is perfect, restoring the soul. "To the law and to the testimony: if they speak not according to this word, it is because there is no light in them" (Isaiah 8:20).

The law is holy, just and good. The good man will sing, "O send out Thy light and Thy truth: let them lead me, let them bring me unto Thy holy hill" (Psalm 43:3). The Son of God came not to destroy but to fulfill the law, and He said that those who do and teach such things shall be called greatest in the kingdom of heaven. Manifestly, it is the whole law and not just part of it that sets the standard for human behavior. If a man would be perfect as his Father in heaven is perfect, he must love not only his friends but his enemies also. "For whosoever shall keep the whole law, and yet offend in one point, he is guilty of all" (James 2:10).

The law is like a seamless garment; if you tear out any piece, the garment itself is ruined. Or it is like a vase; if you break any part, the vase is broken.

The unconverted person has no respect for the law at all. If, as we have already shown, he hates the Lawgiver, why would he do anything other than hate His law? If he will have nothing to do with God Himself or His messengers, why should he bind himself by His regulations?

Like his father, the devil, who is called "the lawless one," he is never obedient to the will of God intentionally. The men of this world are called in Scripture the "children of disobedience" (Ephesians 2:2, 5:6).

It is true that the unconverted do some things commanded by the law, but they never do these things *because* they are commanded by the law. In fact, they do them *in spite* of the fact that the law commands them. The law says "Thou shalt not steal," and it is true that wicked men generally obey this precept, in that they do not steal everything from everybody all the time. But that is not because God has so commanded it; rather, it is because men will not let him get away with it. It is because honesty pays. Congressional committees can do for some men what conscience will never do, because these men have no fear of God in their eyes but they do fear men—at least, a sufficiently large number of powerful men. They will try to vindicate their corruptions not because they are convicted of sin, but because they have lost face with society. All the so-called morality of unconverted men, and there is much of it, is ultimately of this sort. One thing is certain: their acts are not done out of regard for Someone Whom they do not regard, or for a law which they hate.

As a third point, the Bible condemns men because their *goal* is evil. For an act to be good, it must not only proceed from love in the heart and be regulated by the law of God, but it must also aim at advancing the glory of God. Since God alone is good, being infinitely worthy, independently blessed, and the sum of all virtue, it is clear that He alone is the worthy object of any effort by any creature at any time.

The very first commandment states that we shall have no other gods in His presence. He alone is God, and there is none other. For this reason He is a jealous God. All the gods of this world are idols, less than vanity, the object of the prophets' mockery, the creations of creatures. The only and sovereign God brings all things to pass according to His good pleasure and makes all things to praise Him. The Bible saints rejoice in this fact and desire nothing other than that His will be done. Even with respect to the destinies of men, they say with Jesus, "I thank thee, O Father, Lord of heaven and earth, because thou hast hid these things from the wise and prudent, and hast revealed them unto babes. Even so, Father: for so it seemed good in thy sight" (Matthew 11:26–27).

Unconverted persons never aim at the glory of God. They always promote it, but in spite of themselves, not intentionally. Not only do they not aim at the advancement of God's glory, but they seek to obscure and destroy it. God makes the wrath of men to praise him; but it is the *wrath* of men (Psalm 76:10).

This is the point at which, peculiarly, the line of cleavage between the converted and the unconverted appears. The unconverted can never rest in God as the supreme end of all things; the saint can rest in nothing else. The unconverted take offense that man is not the object of all our striving; the converted rejoice in it. When Auguste Comte, the saying goes, sought for a god, he looked all over the universe and then found it in a mirror. According to the unconverted, the chief end of man is to glorify himself and enjoy himself forever. He cannot come to rest in any other deity, and, like Larry in Maugham's *Razor's Edge*, he wanders over the world until he finds peace in thinking he and God are one. At one conference I spoke with a bright young girl who, when she realized that God was sovereign in the disposition of

all things, said to me, "I was never closer to not being a
Christian." I replied, "You were never closer to being a
Christian." She realized the crucial issue.

Unconverted persons often give the appearance of
being religious and seeking God's glory, but their behavior always turns out to be profound irreligion which
seeks their own glory. This pretense is particularly common in this day of very loose church membership.
Consider the following instance.

A couple who are having marital difficulties pass a
church bulletin board. There they read, "They who pray
together stay together." They say to themselves, "Perhaps
that is the trouble with our marriage: we have not prayed
together. Perhaps we should try this; maybe it will save
our marriage." This is their conversion. But it is a conversion from one form of error to another; they are driving our one devil and making room for seven more. There
is no conviction of sin against God, only a sense that they
have engaged in bad judgment to their own detriment.

So they change from a prayerless life to a prayerful
life. But why? Because they love God? No, because they
love themselves and their marriage. Do they now pray to
God as God? No, they pray to a flunky whom they are
trying out to see if he can salvage the mess they made of
their marriage. Do they say "Speak, Lord, for Thy servants hear"? No, they say, "Listen, Lord, we have a job for
You." They still hate God—a sovereign God, anyhow—
and will come to terms only with a figment of their
imagination who will do their bidding.

The god to whom they are praying is not their
Creator; he is their creation. The god to whom they pray
is not their God; they are his. He does not use them or tell
them what to do; they use him and tell him. They are the

gods of their own shrine and he is their servant.

So they have religion. And it works. They testify to its success. Their last condition is worse than the first. Because at first, when there was only one devil, they knew they didn't have any religion and there was always hope that they would be convicted of sin and converted. But now, alas, they have religion and are immune to true conversion.

Part 5

Conclusion

Chapter 25

The Pragmatic Test

Christianity insists on strict morality. Man was not made for morals, but morals for man. Man is a true man, in the fullest sense, only as he is a moral man. The image of God which he bears is a natural and a moral image. When he loses the moral image, retaining only the natural one, he becomes a devil and no longer a true man. Consequently, sanctification, or the process of becoming holy, is a work of God's free grace whereby we are renewed in the whole man after the image of God and are enabled more and more to die unto sin and live unto righteousness. There is no other way to be happy but to trust and obey.

Nor it is happiness alone which depends on one's morality; our destiny also is related to it. A man once said he had stolen one electric light bulb and screwed it into the ceiling of his room. Each time he prayed, looking up toward heaven, he saw that stolen bulb and suffered torments of conscience. Finally he could stand it no longer and returned the bulb. Later, commenting on this experience, the man said, "If I had not returned the bulb I would have gone to heaven anyway, but I would not have been happy along the way." It is true that he would not have been happy along the way, but neither would he have gone to heaven. The Word of God says that thieves shall not enter the kingdom of God. It does not specify how much a person must steal in order to become a thief. Presumably, anyone who takes something that does not belong to him qualifies as a thief if he does not return it. And if he is a thief, he is not on his way to heaven. Hence morality, while it is not the meritorious basis of salvation, is an indispensable accompaniment of it. Without it, a man will never be happy either in this world or in the next.

So the way to life is straight and narrow. It is not crowded. Too much self-denial, and crucifixion of lust, and turning from the world, and doing difficult good things are required of those who would enter and stay on this road of life. But still it is the only road to life. The other road is broad, with room for all sorts and species of men and sinners. It requires nothing, but it leads nowhere but to destruction.

It may be most in order, by way of conclusion, to quote Hawthorne's parody of *Pilgrim's Progress*:

"In the City of Destruction he was taken charge of by a man named Mr. Smooth-it-Away, who explained that the old way to the Celestial City was too long and hard and rough, and that very few pilgrims went that way any more. Instead they took the train on the railroad that had been built for them from the very heart of the City of Destruction to the Celestial City. So he boarded the train and walked through it. It was filled with people he was surprised to find there, men and women who had made no pretense of faith or practice, and who openly scorned at the beliefs of their fathers and mothers. They were on the train setting out for the Celestial City as lively as if they were away on a summer excursion. He was rather shocked to learn that Apollyon, the old enemy of the faithful, was the engineer in charge of the train. But he was told that

Apollyon was really a very good fellow, and inasmuch as he was an excellent engineer, he had been engaged for this work.

"He asked for Mr. Greatheart, the former guide of pilgrims. He was advised that Greatheart had grown so preposterously stiff and narrow, and was in such constant trouble with the management of the road, that they had had to let him go.

"The train started. It crossed the Slough of Despond on a bridge. A tunnel had been cut through the Hill of Difficulty, and the material from the excavation had been utilized to fill up the Valley of Humiliation.

"They thundered into the Valley of the Shadow. It was no longer the dark and dreadful place of yore. Gas lights set along the track illumined it from end to end. They came to Vanity Fair, formerly dreaded and shunned by pilgrims. There the train stopped for a long halt, in order that the passengers might enjoy themselves.

"They went on again. Now and then they would pass pilgrims toiling wearily along the old road. They liked to raise the windows and jeer as they passed. They came to the Delectable Mountains and along the borders of Beulah Land, and at length to the brink of the river. There in the slip was a steam ferryboat to take them to the Celestial City. The passengers grew a little uneasy as they beheld the river, and more so when they looked into the faces of the men who were to carry them over. The boat started and then they saw that its prow was turned, not toward the Celestial City, but toward the darkness and the abyss. Then there were cries and consternation. But it was too late."

This book is not the narrow road, the ethical way to life; it is merely a map of that road. It does not bring life; it only indicates where life may be found. A person may memorize this volume and be as dead and immoral as when he began. This book has never claimed it could bring life; it has aimed only to point out the way of life and to give some reasons for duty. If the reasons are cogent, we are saying compellingly to our readers: "Here is the way, walk ye in it."